# Rock climbing

**Pete Livesey**

**Springfield Books Limited**

Published by Springfield Books Limited
Norman Road, Denby Dale
Huddersfield HD8 8TH, West Yorkshire
England

First edition 1989

**Erratum**
The material on page 43 should
be on page 47, and vice versa.

Acknowledgements

Design: Douglas Martin
Photography: unless otherwise
acknowledged, all photos are by the
author
Illustrations: Barry Davies
Typesetting: Armitage Typo/Graphics,
Huddersfield
Printed and bound in England by Butler
and Tanner Ltd, Frome, Somerset
The author and publishers are grateful to
the following for permission to include
copyright photographs:John Beatty: page
18 (left)
Ian Horrocks: pages 35 (left), 72, 107 (left),
115 (left), 125 and 143 (top right)
Bernard Newman: pages 17 and 35 (right)

Cover picture: Mick Lovatt on Rude Boys,
Smith Rock, Oregon
(Photo: Ian Horrocks)
Frontispiece: South Ridge of the
Salbitschijen, Switzerland

British Library Cataloguing in
Publication Data

Livesey, Pete
Rock climbing
1. Rock climbing – manuals
I. Title
796.5'223

ISBN 0-947655-48-4

# Contents

1 **About rock climbing** · *page 9*

What is rock climbing?      *page 10*
Safety: an important note      *page 13*

2 **Starting climbing** · *page 14*

Breaking out on your own      *page 16*

3 **Tackling a climb** · *page 19*

Single-pitch climbs      *page 19*
Multi-pitch climbs      *page 20*

4 **Clothing and equipment** · *page 23*

Clothing      *page 23*
Footwear      *page 25*
Helmets      *page 27*
Harnesses      *page 28*
The rope      *page 29*
Slings, krabs, nuts and other bits      *page 31*

5 **Ropecraft** · *page 39*

Knots      *page 39*
Coiling and uncoiling the rope      *page 42*
Anchoring      *page 43*
Stances      *page 45*
Belaying      *page 45*
The rope in leading      *page 47*
Climbing calls      *page 48*
The art of belaying      *page 48*

6 **Anchors** · *page 50*

Spikes      *page 50*
Blocks      *page 51*
Thread belays      *page 51*
Trees      *page 52*
Pitons      *page 52*
Nuts      *page 56*
Bolts      *page 57*
Connecting the anchor to the belayer      *page 57*

7 **Climbing techniques** · **part one** · *page 58*

Handholds and footholds      *page 59*
Moving on rock      *page 63*

| 8 | **Climbing techniques · *part two* ·** *page 66* | Slabs | page 66 |
| | | Walls | page 67 |
| | | Chimneys | page 67 |
| | | Cracks | page 68 |
| | | Grooves and corners | page 74 |
| | | Roofs and overhangs | page 75 |
| 9 | **Leading · *part one* ·** *page 76* | Leading qualities | page 77 |
| | | Guidebooks and guides | page 77 |
| | | Route finding | page 78 |
| | | Protection | page 80 |
| | | Learning to lead | page 81 |
| 10 | **Leading · *part two* ·** *page 82* | Protection techniques | page 82 |
| | | Equipment and carrying it | page 82 |
| | | Spacing of nuts | page 84 |
| | | Runner strength | page 85 |
| | | Placing protection | page 86 |
| | | Rope systems | page 93 |
| 11 | **Training for climbing ·** *page 99* | General principles | page 99 |
| | | Components of climbing performance | page 100 |
| | | Training methods | page 102 |
| | | Training regimes | page 110 |
| | | Mental training | page 111 |
| 12 | **Advanced techniques ·** *page 116* | Efficient movement | page 116 |
| | | Tiny or poor holds | page 120 |
| | | Levitation | page 121 |
| 13 | **Competition climbing ·** *page 124* | Competition rules and procedures | page 127 |
| | | Training for competitions | page 128 |
| | | Competition strategies | page 129 |
| 14 | **Self rescue ·** *page 131* | Abseiling or rappelling | page 131 |
| | | Prussiking | page 135 |
| | | Dealing with problems | page 136 |
| 15 | **The environment and ethics ·** *page 140* | The climber and the wilderness | page 141 |
| | | Access to routes | page 141 |
| | | Climbing ethics | page 142 |
| | | New routes | page 145 |
| | | Soloing | page 145 |
| 16 | **What now? ·** *page 146* | Where to climb | page 146 |

**17**  **Information and organisations** · *page 155*

*The British Mountaineering Council*  page 155
*Climbing courses*  page 155
*Books, guidebooks and magazines*  page 155

**18**  **Climbing terms and grades** · *page 157*

*Ropework*  page 157
*Equipment*  page 157
*Rock and its features*  page 158
*Climbing moves*  page 159
*Grades of climbs*  page 159

Ron Fawcett on the first ascent of
Crack-a-Go-Go, Yosemite Valley

# 1 *About rock climbing*

This book is about the sport of rock climbing – but the fascination, challenge and thrills of the sport cannot be adequately described in any book. You may get some idea of why people climb from these pages, but the only people who really know are the rock climbers themselves.

Changing society has in recent years influenced a move away from traditional sports and games to the less structured, freer, world of the outdoors where excitement and adventure are to be found in environments of great beauty and stimulation. Rock climbing is one such activity. Various factors contribute to its attraction as a sport: it requires elements of skill, physical challenge, judgement and determination, risk and danger, competition and always an appreciation of the environment. Of these aspects it is probably those of risk and danger which are most obvious to the public. In fact the skill and judgement of the rock climber is used to minimise the danger and finely control the risk, but these features are inevitably always present. For that reason it would be irresponsible to promote rock climbing as an activity for everyone, and this book is not intended to do so. Its aim is to try and help those who know they want to take up rock climbing and those who are already rock climbers by offering information and advice on equipment, techniques and the scope of the activity. This book will help you to develop skill, style, judgement and experience without the ignorance that can lead to disaster.

You can learn to play chess or learn the rules of football from a book in your armchair, but you cannot learn to rock climb from there. Every situation in rock climbing is different, every piece of rock, every move, every change in weather demands a different kind of action. This can only be learnt by building up your experience in a practical situation, preferably with someone more experienced than yourself. If you ask the great rock climbers of today how they started climbing they almost always tell some horrific tale of epics with their mother's clothes line, but they will also mention some more experienced friend or acquaintance who gave the necessary help to set them in the right direction.

Read on and enjoy your climbing.

*The magic of rock: the granite domes of the High Sierra, California*

## WHAT IS ROCK CLIMBING?

Although this book is about the sport of rock climbing it must always be remembered that rock climbing is only a part of the greater sport of mountaineering, with all the extra qualities that activity demands. Knowledge of navigation, survival techniques and hostile weather equipment, an exploratory instinct, the ability to keep going for several days in adverse conditions and a knowledge of snow and ice climbing are but a few of the qualities required a modern mountaineer.

Rock climbing grew as a separate sport partly because many people living in non-mountainous areas had neither the funds, time nor inclination to make the journey to the high mountains. For them rock climbing was the answer, a sport that offered so many of the rewards and challenges of mountaineering. The techniques in this book apply equally well to rock climbing whether it be done for its own sake or as a way up a difficult section of some alpine face. The equipment used and the seriousness of the situation can be very different, however. The equipment recommended in this book is for rock climbing only and is frequently inappropriate in a high mountain situation.

Rock climbing techniques were originally developed by mountaineers in order to overcome rock faces during ascents of alpine peaks. Back at home they practised these techniques on the lower crags and cliffs. By the end of the last century rock climbing as a sport in its own right had grown out of these practice sessions on low-lying crags. Gullies and chimneys were the first climbing problems to be attacked, later came slab and ridge climbing, and now all of these plus the steepest walls, cracks and overhangs are fair game for the climber.

Although the techniques and equipment used by rock climbers have changed much since the start of the sport, the attitudes of the original sporting rock climbers are to a large extent reflected in today's rock climber. What are these qualities that have lasted so long through great changes in climbing techniques and standards, and why are they worth preserving? Above all, the climber is out to test his own skill, judgement and ability, and he tries to do this by climbing the rock in as natural a way as possible. The less equipment and outside help he uses, the better – his own satisfaction at conquering the climb from his own resources is so much the greater. A climber could cover a route in pitons for extra handholds and protection but this would only serve to reduce the difficulty of the climb to his own level, damage the rock, and so spoil its challenge for those following. Far better to leave the climb as it was and try something easier.

Climbers will talk of different forms of rock climbing such as 'bouldering', 'crag climbing' or 'big wall climbing'. These can be thought of as different games within the sport of rock climbing, though there is really no clear-cut dividing line between them.

Bouldering takes place on small outcrops or boulders where the climber is rarely more than jumping-off distance from the ground. Equipment is kept to a minimum, light clothing and rock climbing boots being all that is required. This kind of climbing on boulders can be very gymnastic and serves as excellent training for the more difficult moves on bigger climbs. However, climbing on boulders tends to be very 'artificial'. This means that the climbs do not follow natural lines of weakness up the rock as do most routes on bigger cliffs; here the climbs take very artificially contrived combinations of holds to make very hard rock climbing problems. Because of the demand for new and harder routes on the bigger cliffs, many of the new routes there are artificial in line also. Bouldering is an excellent activity for summer evenings when there is not enough time to visit the larger crags; techniques and strength can be developed here while the minimal

*Bouldering on a gritstone boulder: Cow and Calf Rocks, Ilkley*

equipment needed gives a greater sense of freedom. Indeed, some climbers find bouldering so absorbing that they rarely climb on the bigger crags; 'ten-foot tigers', they are called! For most, however, bouldering is only practice for crag climbing.

Crag climbing can be of two types, single-pitch climbs and multi-pitch climbs. Single-pitch climbs are those climbed in one section without the need to stop in the middle to bring up the second man. Most of the outcrops close to our cities have single-pitch climbs

and these are ideal routes for the novice to try. It is here that most developments in rock climbing take place, where new techniques and new degrees of difficulty are first seen; these small outcrops are also where most training (both for techniques and fitness) takes place when the weather permits. Such has been the development and change in climbing style in recent years that it is now true to say that most difficult climbing on outcrops resembles 'bouldering' in approach – you spend days on a climb repeatedly trying, and falling off, each move until the whole climb can be accomplished.

Multi-pitch climbs on the bigger mountain crags involve splitting the climb up into natural sections or 'pitches', each one starting and finishing at a suitable ledge where the leader can tie himself to the rock or anchor. He or she then safeguards the second person with the rope, who then climbs to join the leader on the ledge or 'stance'. Multi-pitch climbs involve extra skills not normally required on the shorter climbs and boulders. Route-finding up a big area of rock and familiarity with all kinds of ropework, both to tackle the climb and get out of difficulty should problems arise, are just two of the techniques required for this kind of climbing. Perhaps it is these extra demands on the climber that make the multi-pitch climb the most popular of the rock-climbing games, there being so much more enjoyment and

11

climbing and many skills of mountaineering. The big wall is usually to be found in a fine remote mountain setting, involving exciting and challenging journeys just to reach the foot of the face . . . an all-round adventure.

Rock climbing is not just about different games, though; it is also about people and their reasons for climbing. It is important to remember that the person who climbs primarily to be in mountains or because they like to move over pleasant expanses of rock is just as important in rock climbing as the hot shot who climbs mainly because of open competition or inter-personal rivalry usual among top standard rock climbers. It is also true to say that some climbers see 'progress' in climbing simply as going to new places and climbs, while others hold the view that in order to progress, one's standard must improve. Similarly, some climbers wish only to play in one 'game', while others see a gradual progression right through from single-pitch climbs to the ascent of Himalayan peaks.

satisfaction to be had on the bigger crags. It is also true to say that the bigger the cliff the more impressive and inspiring are the surroundings, so adding extra enjoyment to the experience.

'Big wall climbing' is another of the rock-climbing games and as its name suggests it take place only on the world's biggest cliffs. Here, besides all the other rock-climbing problems, the climber has to equip himself and carry enough food and sleeping gear to spend perhaps several days on the wall.

Sometimes hammocks and other sophisticated items of equipment are required, but by way of compensation the placing and use of pitons, bolts and nuts for aid is less frowned upon here than in other climbing games. Because of the scarcity of big walls and the amount of equipment required, this aspect of climbing is less popular than the others; nevertheless many rock climbers aspire to this kind of climbing at some point in their career as it brings together all the skills of rock

*The remote Steinene Rinne pass in Austria's Wilder Kaisegebirge, the access route to dozens of big wall climbs*

## SAFETY: AN IMPORTANT NOTE

Nowhere in this book will you find any list of 'Safety Rules for Rock Climbers'. Many other sports involving some element of danger surround the activity with safety rules to protect the participants. Rock climbers have always felt that the risk and danger involved in climbing was an essential part of the activity, the skill and satisfaction of climbing being concerned with overcoming and regulating the amount of danger involved. Safety rules unfortunately give participants a sense of security when followed which may be false; it would never be possible to say that rock climbing was absolutely safe if a set of rules were followed. Safety in rock climbing is not concerned with rules but with gaining experience, learning correct techniques and careful

mature judgement of the situation and your own ability and techniques. The successful climber knows how to control the amount of risk present in rock climbing without eliminating the excitement in the activity completely. The reader should consider every aspect of climbing covered in this book as important in the safety of the activity. Some points will be emphasised as being especially important to the climber's safety — belaying, protection, selection of anchors and judgement of abilities being the most important.

Perhaps more important than a thorough knowledge of the techniques and skills of climbing is the acquisition and gradual accumulation of experience, best gained in the company of more experienced climbers. Acting as 'second' to a more experienced climber is perhaps the best apprenticeship any young climber can have, especially if the leader encourages and is aware of the potential of his apprentice.

Many of the illustrations in this book are of real rock climbers doing real climbs. You will therefore see many climbers without some particular item of safety equipment — a helmet for instance — because they as individuals have made the decision to climb without it: whereas this book, or indeed any responsible mentor, must recommend that you wear a helmet to prevent head injury.

# 2 Starting climbing

There are many ways to start climbing; all have advantages and disadvantages depending on the needs and age of the novice climber. What is really important is that the beginner should have a strong desire to learn to climb. Anything less will result in half-hearted learning of techniques and style which in turn results in unforeseen accidents as well as a lack of commitment to the ethics of the activity and care of the environment in which it takes place.

Let us assume then that you are bursting with enthusiasm to learn to climb. There are now several well-used routes to becoming a climber. Perhaps the best of all is to become an apprentice to a friend who is already a climber and is older or more experienced. Normally he or she would do all the leading of climbs and at the same time teach you the intricacies of ropework and belaying.

*Instructor and pupils*

Alongside this instruction you will be building up experience of different climbing situations until your mentor decides you are ready to lead. That is when you become a climber in your own right; the decisions are now yours. The considerate tutor will always be watching his apprentice, encouraging him to make as many of his own judgements as possible, so helping him towards his début as a lead climber.

If you are not fortunate enough to know an experienced climber who is willing to take you under his wing, then perhaps the next best thing is to go along to your local climbing club. Addresses can normally be obtained from climbing magazines (see pages 155-156). In many clubs there are usually a few people willing to teach a young beginner to climb, and after that you will probably find a regular climbing partner in the club. The beginner may well find that in many clubs there seems to be a barrier between the established members and any newcomers. Enthusiasm and eagerness to learn are the sure ways to break down these barriers. It is often said that club members climb at the standard of the rest of the club; in other words, if you join an easy-going club where the climbing standard is fairly low, then you are unlikely to progress beyond that standard yourself. There is certainly a lot of truth in this theory, but if you are aware of the problem then you can look for

another club or a climbing partner who also wishes to progress further.

The majority of climbers these days don't belong to a club, however, or at least not a formal one, but are more likely to belong to a loose-knit band of climbing friends centred around some crag, climbing area or even bar. In the absence of clubs, just appearing regularly at a crag or climbing wall may be the only way into the activity.

Many people today start climbing through their school or youth organisation. It is a very handy way of getting an introduction to the activity but it usually has one or two drawbacks. Many teachers and instructors who take children climbing feel restricted by safety regulations and consequently tend to modify the kind of climbing they teach in an effort to remove all the risk. Whilst it can still be said that the young climber enjoys learning a watered-down version of rock climbing, he never experiences the full benefits of the challenge and adventure in real climbing. Too often you will see large groups of children cluttered with unnecessary equipment queueing up to be top-roped by the teacher up a one-pitch outcrop climb. And that is frequently all there is to their rock climbing experience; all the rich experiences gained from choosing a climb, finding the cliff, interpreting the guidebook and the first lead are lost. The good

teacher or instructor will try to avoid changing the nature of rock climbing and will be mindful of the needs of the progressive young climber. As soon as a young climber shows signs of progressing further than the normal school situation will allow,

*The young beginner*

then the teacher should introduce him to a suitable club that will allow him to progress and so continue to be challenged by climbing. There are now scores of outdoor centres and commercial organisations up and down the country offering rock climbing courses at most levels. Some are private organisations, others are state funded. The cost and quality of these courses vary tremendously; but there is unfortunately no means at present to help the beginner discriminate between good and bad courses. Most courses are advertised in the climbing magazines (see pages 155-156).

A question here about all the advice on starting to climb. How do you know if your leader or instructor is any good? It would be very easy to learn a set of highly dangerous techniques from an incompetent but friendly leader. You must watch him and compare him with other climbers around; is he as good, and does he look as skilful and slick when arranging his belays? Do other climbers avoid him? You must ask yourself these questions; only professional climbers and guides hold formal qualifications, friends or teachers are very unlikely to do so.

## BREAKING OUT ON YOUR OWN

You will not learn everything from your leader or instructor – and anyway sooner or later you will realise that much more satisfaction is to be gained from breaking away and climbing with a friend. Much of what you can learn from your instructor is no good without practice; in your own time you can practise ropework and belay techniques. Small cliffs, boulders or climbing walls near your home are ideal for practising and improving your climbing skills. If by now you have a climbing partner you are ready for your own climbing trips. Ideally, of course, your first climbing partner should be more experienced than yourself and do most of the leading until you are ready to lead. This is often not possible, but if you have learnt to lead with your instructor and he is confident of your techniques, then you should be ready to be a leader in your own right.

*A busy gritstone outcrop – an ideal place to meet other climbers*

*Martin Berzins on Ice Spurt Special,
Kilnsey, North Yorkshire*

*Necronomicon, Verdon Gorge, France*

*Jill Lawrence on the Rotgarten,*
*Rheinland-Pfalz, West Germany*

# 3 *Tackling a climb*

Just how do climbers tackle a single-pitch or multi-pitch climb? What use do they make of the rope, how does it help the leader? This chapter sets out to answer these questions.

## SINGLE-PITCH CLIMBS

### Top roping

On many small crags, especially with beginners, it is common practice to 'top rope' climbs. This simply means that the belayer walks to the top of the crag, anchors, lowers a rope to the second(s) below who then climbs while belayed from above. A popular variation of this system is for an anchor to be fixed at the top of the crag (or indeed part way up); the rope is run from the second on the ground up to the krab on the anchor, through it, and back down to the belayer who is also on the ground. When the climber reaches the anchor he simply puts his weight on the rope and is lowered back to the ground. Using this variation the belayer can see all that is going on and offer advice to the climber.

A and B tie on to opposite ends of the rope and B anchors himself at the foot of the cliff. He then belays the rope for A as he starts the climb. Should A fall and tumble down the hillside B will be able to hold him with a friction device (belay plate) attached to his harness.

A has now passed a suitable place to fix a running belay, which he connects to the main climbing rope with a karabiner. If he falls now his flight will soon be stopped by B as he drops below the running belay ('runner' for short)

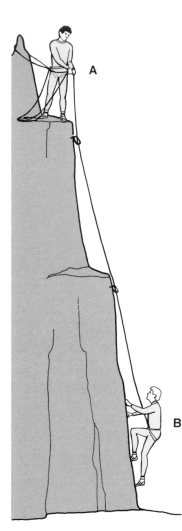

Many crags and cliffs are too high or complex for the climb to be done in one pitch or stage. The rope may not be long enough; a particular section of climbing may be broken naturally by large ledges or the climbing may be particularly intricate, involving lots of changes of direction which causes rope drag. All are reasons for breaking a climb up into pitches; another equally common reason is that you get a rest after each pitch so a particularly strenuous climb may be made easier that way.

## Multi-Pitch Climbs

On this cliff the climb must be done in several stages as the rope is not long enough for the climb to be completed in one pitch.

Ledges or comfortable sitting down spots are picked out for 'stances' at the ends of pitches. In our example the first pitch is short and has no protection (i.e. no places to put runners), so it is pointless for the second (B) to anchor himself. If the ground below the climb were sloping then B would anchor himself to prevent either or both climbers tumbling down the slope. Here B is

not anchored, but he still pays out the rope carefully and should A find a place for a runner, B could still hold a fall on that runner quite effectively.

A is now anchored on the first stance and he is belaying B as he climbs the pitch. At the ledge B takes the rack from A and starts to lead the next pitch, with A still belaying. This is called 'leading through' when the leads are swapped on each pitch.

A has now reached the top and selected suitable anchors to tie himself on with. He then belays the rope so that B can take his belay off, remove the anchors and begin to climb. As he climbs he removes the runners left in by A. If B should slip his fall is arrested immediately by A at the top, who takes the rope in through a belay plate attached to his harness.

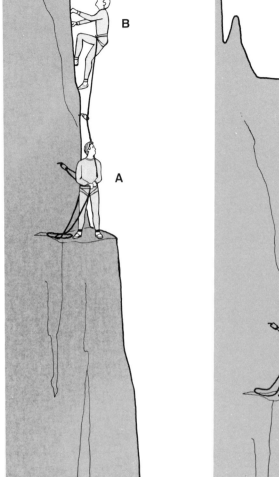

This convenient system needs less ropework and no changing over of anchors at ledges; it is generally much faster than other methods. If B was a novice climber not yet ready to lead then he would have to anchor himself at the first stance to anchors separate from those used by A, if possible. A could then untie his belay and carry on to lead the next pitch.

B is now leading through on pitch 2 and looking around for a good running belay as soon as possible.

B is well up the second pitch now with a good runner in place.

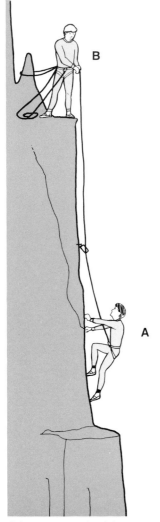

B has now reached the second stance, has anchored himself and is belaying the rope as A climbs to join him, removing the runners as he goes. When A reaches the stance he will take what runners B has left and lead through on to the third pitch, again trying to place a good runner as soon as possible so that any pull on the belayer will be upward. They will continue like this until the top is reached.

# 4  *Clothing and equipment*

Lists of equipment and clothing we must have for climbing, mountaineering or mountain walking are being offered to us all the time. 'Absolutely essential for safety', the posters and pamphlets say. As far as rock climbing is concerned this is just not so; climbers think about equipment in a completely different way. The important thing about rock climbing is that you are accepting a natural challenge, the route up the crag, and the less equipment you use to climb it the more you feel it was just you and the rock. In other words, much of your enjoyment of the climb was because you didn't use lots of mechanical or manufactured aids to get up it. So why have any equipment at all? The answer is complex, but the main reason is that there is a generally accepted level of risk in the activity, and certain safety and protection items are used to keep that risk level acceptable. As well as these items there are what could be called comfort and performance equipment. You will need

comfortable clothing that is warm enough but allows complete freedom of movement, so there is specialist mountain clothing. Performance equipment includes items such as boots or chalk bag which are deliberately designed to enable you to get the best from your physical ability.

Some safety equipment actually hinders climbing performance because it is heavy and cumbersome – helmets for instance. Most equipment, or decisions about what equipment to carry, are a compromise between safety, weight, comfort, performance and keeping within the rules (that is, what is normally acceptable). You could, for instance, carry dozens of krabs, slings, nuts and pegs for protection and be super-safe, but your performance would suffer because of the extra weight and you would spend all your time fiddling about with protection rather than climbing rock. A compromise is therefore arrived at; experts are skilled at making a suitable compromise whereas beginners should always take advice or come down on the side of safety at the expense of performance.

This chapter will mention many of the arguments for and against

various items of equipment, but that is not enough on its own to enable beginners to decide exactly what equipment they should buy. Luckily help is normally on hand at your local climbing shop. I have found that virtually all specialist shops are staffed by climbers of some experience who will offer the beginner sensible advice even if it means missing a sale, and their advice should be sought when deciding, for instance, exactly what boot to buy.

Expense is a problem, of course, especially if you start climbing with the idea of getting fully equipped from the outset. This is probably a mistake anyway; better to start with a few basic items which can then be combined with your partner's equipment to make a full set. It is not necessary to buy full sets of fancy clothing; that will come later on when you get better – tracksuits, sweaters and tee shirts are quite sufficient for a start. Suggestions for recommended gear for beginners are to be found at the end of this chapter. Remember, though, that whilst the equipment described here is 'state of the art' today, it might be improved upon tomorrow!

*The minimalist approach to equipment on a new route in the Zagros Mountains of Iran*

## CLOTHING

Climbing can be very strenuous and athletic when you are actually doing it; conversely it can be very cold, windy and inactive when you are belaying. Clothing therefore needs to be light to save weight; flexible to allow great freedom of movement; warm and windproof for sitting on ledges and not so baggy that it gets in the way or obstructs your vision, of footholds for instance. Most young hot shots would say that clothing needs to be coloured outrageously but this is just part of the ethic. Another quality of clothing that becomes immediately obvious when you do a climb is its slipperiness: smooth slippery clothing such as nylon or plastic waterproofs do nothing to help your adhesion to the rock when trying to wedge in a chimney or scramble on to a ledge, and are best avoided.

Modern climbing clothing is designed on the 'shell' principal which means that the complete outfit is made up of a few layers of clothing, each in itself quite thin and light. New layers are added for each worsening climatic condition. Typically a set of shell clothing for the upper body would consist of a thin wool or polypropylene thermal vest (thin, warm, but on its own allows plenty of ventilation) followed by a thinnish fibre pile jacket or a sweater (these are even warmer and remarkably windproof) and finally a windproof

and possibly showerproof but lightweight jacket. For high mountain crags and very wet conditions where hypothermia is a real problem it is necessary to keep relatively dry with a proofed nylon or Goretex-style cagoule. Here one sacrifices non-slip qualities for the sake of keeping dry. Cagoules also get in the way and so climbers tend to avoid them unless the conditions are really bad or a crag is so far from civilisation or shelter that keeping dry is a priority. Note that while any

one layer of shell clothing may offer excellent freedom of movement, putting all layers together may have a considerable restricting effect. Check this out when trying the clothing on; can you extend your arms upwards in all your clothing with the same ease as you can when wearing only a tee shirt? Similarly, any trousers, tights or layered leg covering should allow you to place your foot as high up the shop wall as you can when wearing shorts. Of all the aspects of flexibility that should be retained

*The modern approach: rock slippers, Lycra tights, harness, chalkbag and 'quick draws' – Mick Ryan in action on Malham Cove, North Yorkshire*

it is leg movement, and particularly knee and foot lift, that is most important; non-restricting leg wear is therefore of paramount importance.

The most popular leg wear nowadays are slim-fitting tracksuit trousers made from fairly thin material or skin-hugging Lycra tights. Both offer excellent freedom of movement, but the tights offer little in the way of warmth or protection from the rock. To wear the garish Lycra tights you need to be a hot shot or rebellious youth and be completely insensitive environmentally. In very hot weather shorts are great to wear but they don't protect your skin on routes that involve body contact with the rock such as wide cracks, chimneys or slips and slides on slabby ground. They are worth it, however, on suitable routes for the sheer joy of having complete freedom of movement. Conversely, in very cold weather fibre pile trousers are much warmer than tights or tracksuit trousers, but they are only made in stretchy material by one or two manufacturers. Finally, mountaineering breeches or salopettes (breeches that have a 'bib and brace' top section and keep your middle covered) are useful on cold or bad weather rock climbs, though the average pure rock climber might never own a pair.

Of course, all the clothing mentioned here is the ideal, and not possessing it need not stop you climbing. Absolutely anything will do so long as it keeps you at the right temperature given the conditions and allows you excellent freedom of movement. If 'making do' with clothes not designed for rock climbing, you should particularly avoid baggy trousers that restrict vision and clothing with drawcords or loose bits that could snag on rock or get caught in equipment.

## FOOTWEAR

Good footwear is probably the most important item of equipment in rock-climbing; it helps to build confidence, enables full use of footholds and certainly increases your enjoyment.

There are dozens of choices of 'rock boots' available these days, but all have several similar features. Rock boots have lightweight leather, suede or leather/canvas uppers, a smooth rubber sole and a deep rubber strip around the bottom edge of the uppers. The boots are slim-fitting, tight lacing and just cover the ankle, though many are cut away at the heel to increase foot mobility. They are ridiculously expensive and the better ones tend to wear out fairly quickly because of the soft rubber composite used for the soles. Another parallel brand of rock-climbing footwear is the rock shoe or slipper. These are either lace-up shoe style or 'slip on' elasticated slipper designs, but both have the same friction rand and sole. Shoes and slippers are more specialised than rock boots and while they offer superb performance on a

*Rock boots, rock shoes and slippers*

narrow range of rock-climbing activities they are not to be recommended for the beginner. The basic requisite of a rock boot is that of performance − it must help you climb at the highest standard possible, and that is the sensible feature that most climbers should look for whether they be experienced or complete beginners. The general purpose, utility, last-for-ever, cheap boot compromises performance and is not worth buying. Performance in rock boots is all about two footwork techniques which are commonly needed on climbs − some climbs require only one of the techniques but many require both. They are the qualities of 'edging' and 'smearing'. Edging is the footwork technique required for positive square-cut or sharp footholds and pockets or holes in the rock. The boot is used sideways on small sharp holds and therefore requires lateral stiffness while for pockets the toe is used and therefore a degree of longitudinal stiffness is required. Smearing is the footwork technique concerned with pure friction and is used where there are no footholds at all or where the footholds are poor, sloping or rounded. Here the boot needs to have a very 'sticky' rubber sole and should be flexible to allow maximum contact between boot and rock.

To a large extent the two requirements of edging and smearing are not complementary: edging requires stiffness to be built

in while smearing requires a flexible sole. Similarly, edging techniques require a hard edge to the rubber of the sole whereas sticky rubber for friction moves is invariably soft. A compromise in design is therefore required, which the best boots seem to manage quite effectively. The climber choosing a boot should decide upon the predominant footwork style of the routes he is likely to climb and buy a boot with that bias in its design. It is worth noting here that boots with a smearing bias, or an out-and-out friction emphasis, tend to encourage sloppy footwork and over-use of the arms, especially when there are proper edging-type holds available. For this reason it is a good idea for beginners to go for a performance boot with a slight 'edging' bias.

Recent advances in the chemical composition and surface texture of the rubber soles of boots have led to 'super sticky' boots (originating in Europe) and 'Stealth' rubber from the United States. Super sticky rubber tends to be very soft but is so sticky that one boot will cling to the underside of the other boot when held in the air. Stealth rubber is claimed to be even stickier and is also designed to maximise the second property of boot adhesion to the rock, that of interlocking. Interlocking is the actual physical conformation of rubber to rock. This bond is broken when the boot slides off by a minute tearing of the rubber structure. Stealth rubber is

therefore fairly hard without compromising stickiness and is finished is such a way as to promote interlocking.

The individual climber can also improve the performance of his boots by getting the correct fit, putting them on properly and keeping the sole clean. Generally speaking, boots should be a tightish fit without socks, or with a thin pair. Bear in mind the fact that some boots (the majority), stretch with use while a few shrink with use. Your store will be able to advise you which does what. Boots should obviously be laced up properly in use so that the boot feels part of the foot rather than allowing the foot to slide about inside the boot. Finally, cleanliness of the sole is very important for performance. Regular washing and brushing of the sole after use is a good idea, as is taking care not to stand on muddy or dusty ground before embarking on the rock-climb. Many climbers carry a small strip of towelling or cloth to stand on and wipe both soles before climbing begins.

Mention must also be made of two other types of footwear, plimsolls and mountain boots. In the absence of funds to buy a pair of rock boots, plimsolls (i.e. cheap canvas rubber-soled shoes) will suffice remarkably well on lower grade climbs. It should be pointed out that many 'training shoes' have either plastic soles (very slippery) or deep treads (which tend to 'roll off' smaller holds) and are therefore not as good as the very inexpensive slipper-type smooth-soled plimsolls if you can find them. Smooth-soled or gently ribbed road running shoes are a reasonable alternative if you already have a pair.

Mountain boots are no longer used for rock climbing unless the rock is mixed with snow and ice, necessitating the use of crampons. Even in cold conditions at high altitude it is possible to rock climb in insulated rock boots which can then be put inside a plastic outer boot with cleated sole for extra insulation on snow and ice work. Rock climbing in stiff mountain boots is an art in itself and should be well practised before being used on mountains.

*A typical modern lightweight climbing helmet*

## HELMETS

The newcomer to climbing cannot fail to notice that most climbers on the crags do not wear helmets, and will also note that many of the climbers pictured in this book are also without helmets. On the other hand all responsible advice, from whatever source, insists that climbers should wear helmets – so what's the problem?

In the late 1960s and 1970s virtually all climbers took to wearing helmets; they were an obvious addition to the safety armoury in that they protected the very vulnerable head against falling stones and, more importantly, offered head protection during falls. It should also be noted that it was during this same period that falling became 'popular', if it can be so described. Before then, falling was considered more or less terminal due to the lack of effective protective equipment and technique – once climbers began falling they began hitting their heads during the descent on ledges and the cliff face itself. As climbing became more and more gymnastic, however, two factors became apparent: first, that helmets were heavy, cumbersome and so annoying that they detracted from performance; and second, that as climbs got harder so the rock got steeper and the chances of hitting one's head during a fall lessened. The use of helmets therefore went into rapid decline among climbers of high standard. Unfortunately most newcomers to the sport will mimic the experts, and this is where the argument about whether to wear a helmet falls down. Easier climbs (all those up to the E graded climbs, in fact) are less steep and therefore more likely to result in contact with the rock during a fall. Similarly, stray pebbles falling from above are more likely to hit those climbing or standing belaying close to the foot of the rock if the route is an easier one.

The message, therefore, is that beginners and those on easier climbs should always wear a helmet – you are much more at risk than the expert. Fortunately, helmet design has grown apace and many new helmets are very light plastic affairs which are nothing like as oppressive as the old fibreglass domes of the past. Alpinists still invariably wear helmets, whatever their standard, as they are at great risk; and there seems no reason why those climbing routes that are less than vertical or well supplied with ledges should not do the same. When one has amassed experience of the potential problems and pushed on to steeper routes a proper personal decision can be made about whether to continue wearing a helmet or not.

There are very few types of helmet on the market; it is probably best to go for a light plastic helmet with a comfortable chin strap and substantial foam padding between cradle and helmet. A U.I.A.A. (Union Internationale des Associations d'Alpinisme) approved helmet, normally designated on the label, ensures a safe design though it may not necessarily be the lightest model. (There is a note on U.I.A.A. standards at the end of this chapter.)

## HARNESSES

Harnesses are now universally accepted as an essential part of a climber's safety and comfort equipment. They perform several important functions.

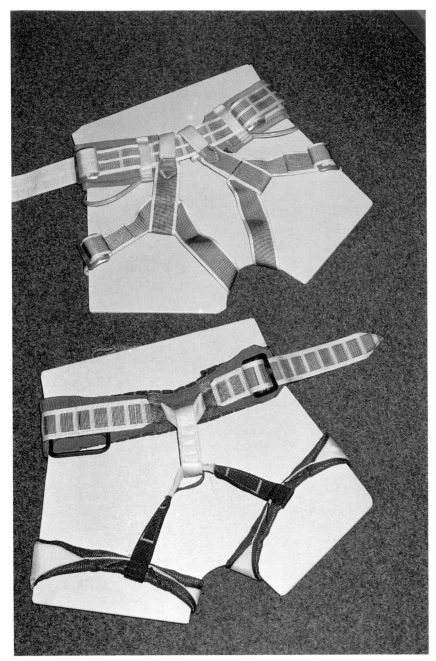

Two harnesses: the upper one requires the rope to be threaded through the upper part of the leg loops while the lower one has a central 'tie-in' loop

- [ ] They transmit the load in a fall to the strongest parts of the body, namely the upper thigh.

- [ ] They spread out the shock loading experienced during a fall by having lots of area in contact with the body.

- [ ] They make dangling on the rope after a fall, or hanging belays, are relatively comfortable procedure.

- [ ] They normally simplify and make safer belaying and abseiling procedures.

- [ ] They provide handy attachment points for other climbing gear such as nuts, krabs and chalk bag.

- [ ] They prevent the climbers capsizing during or after a fall.

The safest harness system is the full body harness or combined 'sit' and chest harness, but both restrict movement and belay procedures to such an extent that they are rarely used by rock climbers. Instead the 'sit harness' is the system almost universally adopted by climbers as being the best combination of safety, weight and convenience.

When choosing a harness there are several features to investigate. The waist belt should be well padded, should have a buckle that does not prise out the lower ribs in a fall and should be adjustable enough to be tightened up properly about the waist. It should not sit about the hips, but on the waist itself, thus alleviating the problems of capsizing and the climber dropping out of the harness if inverted. The leg loops should be comfortable when hanging in the harness and should take the major part of one's weight, but they should also allow total flexibility of movement and not feel restricting. The harness should have an attachment loop that sits at waist level at the front and gear loops in suitable positions (some modern harnesses are of 'do it yourself' design as far as gear loop position goes). Finally, harnesses should have a decent set of instructions on how to adjust them properly and, more importantly, how to anchor and belay with the harness.

## THE ROPE

Every climber should aim to own a rope as soon as possible in his climbing career. Although many clubs will lend beginners a rope, this should be done hesitatingly and great care taken over recording what has happened to it. A rope is obviously crucial to a climber's safety; if you are going to be climbing with a rope then you must have faith in its ability to hold you in a fall. A rope that you have not lovingly cared for since purchase or have borrowed has an unknown history and there is no way of telling just what condition it is in. Accidents occur every year through ropes breaking because they have been allowed to come into contact with oil or battery acid, usually in the boot of a car. Climbing ropes are specially designed to absorb the force put on them by a falling climber. This is obviously their main task and all other qualities of a rope are of secondary importance. The tremendous force that can be exerted by a falling climber would simply break an ordinary rope but the climbing rope stretches and gradually absorbs the energy in the climber's fall. The further the climber falls the more rope he will have between himself and the belay and therefore the more stretch there will be in the rope. This gradual absorbing of the energy means also that there is no sudden force on the climber as there would be if he were jerked to a halt. The force felt by the climber as his fall is arrested is called the 'impact force'; the lower it is the more the rope will stretch and the less chance there is of damage to the climber.

It is very rare for a climbing rope to 'break' in the purest sense of the word; climbing ropes have come apart after contact with damaging chemicals or heat and have been cut in falls where the rope has become taut over a sharp edge of rock. Ropes have also come apart after being worn through by constant local rubbing against the rock, though this is more of a mountaineering problem where fixed ropes are used to regain a high point.

Ropes have several qualities of interest to the climber (apart from modern cosmetic considerations such as matching the rope's colour to one's tights or rock boots!).

☐ Breaking strain – in itself not all that important; all ropes designed for climbing have a sufficient breaking strain, but some are designed for *double* use (a 'half rope') rather than a single one.

☐ Impact force – an important feature related to the 'stretchiness' of a rope. The lower the maximum impact force, the less the likely damage to a climber when the rope arrests his fall.

*11 mm and 9 mm Kernmantel rope*

☐ U.I.A.A. falls – a standardised test in a dynamic situation simulating a falling leader: a rope must pass a minimum number of these severe falls before being awarded the U.I.A.A. standard. Many ropes perform considerably better than the minimum.

☐ Diameter and weight – are important and related features. Ropes intended for single use are normally 11 mm in diameter while double-use ropes are about 9 mm in diameter and obviously considerably lighter. A recent

trend for lighter ropes has resulted in diameters of 10.5 mm and 8.5 mm respectively, with a consequent reduction in breaking strain (bad), impact force (good) and U.I.A.A. fall resistance (bad).

☐ Handling properties – ropes vary considerably in their feel; some are slippery and difficult to knot, others tend to kink easily, while some are very soft and pliant. Most climbers seem to prefer the latter. Bear in mind also that ropes have a habit of changing their handling characteristics with use – ask at your friendly knowledgeable

climbing store about specific brands.

☐ Length – the standard length of rope is either 45 m or 50 m. The former is sufficient for most easy climbing situations whereas the latter length is favoured by alpinists and those venturing on to big rock faces.

Ropes are of Kernmantel construction, which means that they have a woven outer sheath and lightly twisted bundles of continous fibres inside. It is this construction that ensures elasticity and hence an acceptably low impact force.

Ropes should be cared for meticulously, both to prolong their useful life and more importantly to prevent contact with invisible agents of destruction. The first and most obvious point is that falls damage a rope – the U.I.A.A. test establishes that fact. A severe fall (i.e. a fall factor of 2 – see page 98) will damage a rope irreversibly and the rope should probably be discarded after such a fall. It will in any case have lost much of its elasticity, resulting in a higher impact force. Other fall damage may occur during any fall but can be determined visually. A fall over a sharp edge will result in a cut or severe abrasion to the sheath, while a loaded rope running over a loaded static rope will result in severe melting of the static rope. With local damage the offending section can be cut out and the rope used in shortened version for short single-pitch work.

Dirt, sand and grit can get into a rope with use in dirty, sandy situations and by being trodden upon. Don't tread on ropes, and wash them thoroughly in warm water with some fabric softener. This will not remove all the sand and grit but will prolong the life of the rope by lessening damage by internal abrasion caused by the sand. The surface of the rope gets worn and furry-looking in use, and while this is not serious on its own, it does indicate the possible existence of internal damage – in other words, a very furry rope is about ready for replacement.

Ropes should be kept away from flames and other very hot objects, though melting can be seen. Much worse is contact with acid (car batteries for instance) or chemicals such as petroleums where the damage is invisible and terminal. A further cause of deterioration is ultra-violet radiation in sunlight. Ropes should not be stored for long periods in direct sunlight as this will eventually weaken the rope drastically.

When it comes to answering the question 'how long will a rope last', no specific advice can be given because there are so many unknowns in the equation. Perhaps it's best to say that if you climb regularly then you shouldn't expect your rope to last much longer than two or three years.

## SLINGS, KRABS, NUTS AND OTHER BITS

### Slings

Slings are nowadays almost exclusively constructed of lengths of flat tape sewn into loops. They have a variety of uses, but their main function is in anchoring and protection where a sling needs to be put around or over a natural spike of rock or chokestone jammed in a crack. A krab is then used to connect the sling to the main rope or direct to the belayer's harness. Slings are also used to lengthen other runners to minimise rope drag caused when the main rope zig-zags too much.

Tape is used in preference to short knotted loops of climbing rope because it lies on the rock better and is thus less likely to roll off or work loose. It is also lighter, easier to handle and less likely to be cut over sharp edges.

In the past it was necessary to use 25 mm wide tape with a breaking strain of around 2400 kg in order to ensure a 'safety chain' (see page 49) of consistent strength. New materials and tape construction now enable tape loops of the same 2400 kg breaking strain to use 15 mm tape with a consequent saving in weight and bulk. A 15 mm tape is also better with modern lightweight krabs because the load transmitted through the tape to the krab is concentrated on the strongest part of the krab. Wider tapes can spread the load out and this weakens the krab. It is normal to have one 'double sling' of 120 cm loop length for large spikes and blocks; two or three 'single slings' of 60 cm length for smaller spikes: two or three 45 cm slings for extending runners: and several short loops of between 10 and 30 cm for clipping into fixed protection or extension. The latter are called 'quick draws' and are carried with a krab at either end for fast use.

Like the accessory cord used for threading nuts, tape has a high static breaking strain but little elasticity and should therefore not

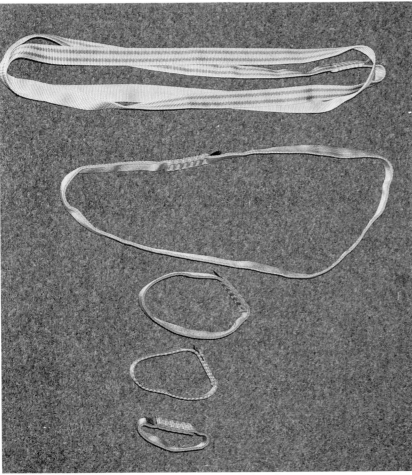

*A double tape, single tape and selection of 'quick draws'*

shut, and screwgate krabs with a sleeve that screws or slides over the gate thus locking it closed. Krabs are made from aluminium alloy bars of various thicknesses, resulting in krabs of different strengths and weight. Snaplink krabs are used for connecting runners to the climbing rope or for extending runners and use on quick draws. Very light snaplinks are used where runners appear frequently, requiring lots of krabs to be carried, and on climbs where lots of runners are used (mostly the harder routes), the shock loading on any one krab in a system of runners is likely to be low, so the weaker lightweight krabs are therefore appropriate. Heavier snaplinks are normal on easy climbs where there may be longer fall potential due to a lower availability of runner placements, or more probably less expertise in finding placements. Lightweight krabs have breaking strains of 1800 to 2000 kg while the heavier models should be rated 2200 kg or above. Screwgate krabs are used for connections at main anchors or stances, for connecting harness to rope and belay plate or descendeur to harness. In these situations an inadvertently unclipped rope could be fatal for both climbers − an occurrence that a properly locked screwgate krab prevents.

Other krab features to watch out for are ease of gate opening − not too stiff or they will be impossible to use in desperate situations, but not

be used in place of a climbing rope, since the very high impact loads that they generate would easily damage the climber and might even break the rope or tape.

### Krabs

Karabiners, shortened to 'krabs' (U.K.) or 'biners' (U.S.A.), are used for connecting runners to the 'running' rope and anchors to a static rope or direct to the harness. On some harnesses a krab is also used to connect the harness to the end of the rope, while krabs also form an essential component of belay plate systems.

There are two basic types, snaplink or ordinary krabs with a spring-loaded gate that snaps

*A selection of krabs with two screwgate krabs on the right*

too light or they are likely to unclip themselves. Check the mechanical bits of the krab and both ends of the gate – the sharp edges should be well smoothed off to prevent snagging on ropes and clothing. A krab should also be capable of being opened when loaded with the climber's weight so that ropes and slings etc. can be clipped or unclipped during emergency procedures.

## Nuts

'Nuts' is the collective term for all removable and environmentally friendly pieces of hardware that are put in cracks or holes for protection and anchoring. They are of three main types: chocks or wedges of aluminium or brass; hexagonal camming nuts (called hexes or polys); and expandable

*A typical nut selection*

camming devices where the nut expands to fit the crack size.

Chocks and wedges are, as the name implies, wedge-shaped chunks of aluminium (sometimes brass in very small sizes) varying in width from 1.5 mm to 30 mm. Most are tapered on all four faces and can therefore be turned sideways to fit a larger crack. Many modern

wedges have sculptured faces that detract from the symmetry but enhance placement possibilities and the holding power of the nut in difficult or marginal situations. Smaller wedges are threaded with a flexible wire cable that is much stronger than accessory cord of the same diameter but is rather stiff compared with cord and invariably needs connecting to the main rope with a flexible link such as a quick draw. Once the nut is large enough to accept 5.5 mm accessory cords then modern high-strength materials such as Spectra or Kevlar can be used, which gives a 2500 kg breaking strain for a loop of cord.

Wedges are normally sold already wired in the small sizes. Accessory cord loops on nuts should be kept reasonably short, about 20–25 cm loop length, and the cords should be colour coded according to nut size. It is always

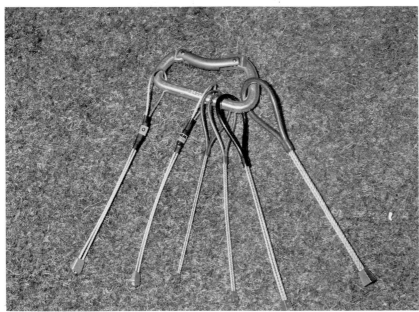

*Small wired nuts*

with reasonable security in almost parallel cracks. Hexes have a larger size range than wedges, starting at approximately 15 mm and going up to 90 mm or so. Some of the smaller sizes are wired, but the stiffness of the wire prevents the camming operation from working properly in most cracks.

Expanding cam devices are complicated mechanical contraptions (compared to the simplicity of wedges, anyway) consisting of a stem or wire fastened to a spindle. On the spindle, and usually spring-loaded, are anything from one to four cams which expand to fit the crack perfectly. When a load is applied the cams try to expand further, thus securing the device even more firmly. They are the only

possible to extend a nut loop with a quick draw but very awkward to shorten one.

Always take note of the breaking strain of the wire loop on smaller nuts – it will invariably be the weak link in a safety chain; some of the smallest nuts will only stand a fall of a metre or so even in low fall factor situations (see page 98).

Hexes are hollow tubular nuts of an irregular hexagonal shape giving two alternative widths when used normally and a third size when used endways in a crack. In the two normal positions it will be noted that the cord loop does not hang vertically, but is displaced sideways. When a load is applied to the loop in a fall the cord twists the nut (camming), causing it to jam more firmly in the crack. This feature enables hexes to be placed

*Expanding cam devices*

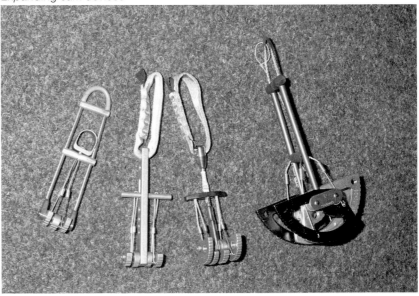

Chris Plant on The Cad,
North Stack Wall

John Dunne on the first ascent of New
Statesman, Cow and Calf Rocks, Ilkley

*Nicko Mailander on Voie Directissime,*
*Buis les Baronnies, France*

nut that works reasonably well in outward flaring cracks or perfectly parallel cracks. They are very expensive and can be difficult to remove due to their habit of 'walking' into the depths of cracks when a shaking climbing rope moves them – though removal tools are available. Those with flexible stems are stronger in situations when the stem sticks out of the crack (especially in horizontal cracks) but are slightly more difficult to remove. Expanding cam devices are available in a range suitable for cracks from 12 mm to 100 mm in width.

## Other bits of hardware

Perhaps the most essential additional accessory is some form of belaying device. This is a kind of friction lock that aids the task of holding and lowering a fallen colleague. One could use a running knot on a krab for this, such as an Italian hitch, or a multi-purpose device such as a figure '8' descendeur, but by far the most common and effective device is the belay plate. A belay plate (frequently called a Sticht plate after the inventor) is a circular piece of aluminium plate with one or two slots for single or double rope systems. A 'bight' of rope (a doubled piece of rope) is pushed through the slot and clipped into a karabiner which is in turn attached to the harness or directly to an

anchor. In a fall the plate is forced against the krab, creating sharp bends and therefore high friction in the running rope; the fall is therefore arrested. For the beginner this item is as important as helmet, harness and boots.

Abseil devices, or descendeurs, are common items of equipment and are of several different types. Like the belay plate they all work on the principle of introducing friction to the sliding rope (or rather sliding climber in this case) by bending the rope around some device. Descendeurs vary tremendously in their safety characteristics – some are downright dangerous. If you must have one then the figure of eight descendeur has several fail-safe qualities, though even it has problems in use. A belay plate, however, doubles as a perfectly acceptable descendeur, or an Italian hitch or karabiner brake system can be used.

Most ambitious climbers will acquire a chalk bag at some stage of their progress. 'Chalk', blocks of magnesium carbonate, is used to dry hands, and fingers especially, of sweat and so increase friction on hand and finger holds. It wears off quickly and must be reapplied, hence the need for a small 'hand-sized' bag to carry the chalk. Typical chalk bag features are a pile lining to hold the chalk and ensure a rapid even dusting; a stiffened opening to keep the bag open and a flap, drawcord or flexible centre section to prevent

chalk spilling when the bag is tipped upside down during exciting moves. The chalk is gymnastics chalk, through special 'climbing chalk' is now available in powder form – some is even coloured to match the rock colour.

There is considerable ethical debate about the use of chalk; it certainly works and can improve performance dramatically in

*The Sticht plate in use*

certain circumstances, but its use is criticised on two main counts. First, it is an artificial aid and one can climb without it – the general consensus seems to be that it shouldn't be used on easy routes that were originally climbed in pre-chalk days but its use is acceptable on hard routes. There is also an environmental objection in that chalk defaces the rock quite dramatically on dark-coloured rocks and in sheltered overhanging situations where rain does not wash the chalk off. Also important is the issue of route 'marking' whereby routes climbed with chalk have more or less permanently marked handholds which can be seen from afar, thus removing a key enjoyment in climbing, that of discovering the holds, sequence and route for oneself. There is no answer to the problem but a conservative approach to the use of chalk will help – use little, and only where necessary; use coloured chalk appropriate to the rock colours; and consider brushing chalk off routes after heavy use.

## Equipment and weight – what to carry

Here is an experiment to try: dress in climbing clothes only, find a pull-up bar and count how many pull-ups you can do in one continuous session or (better) in five minutes. Repeat the exercise twenty-four hours later, but this time wear helmet, harness, chalk bag, six slings and krabs, ten quick draws (each with two krabs), a rack of nuts and krabs and a belay plate with screwgate krab. You should also hang a coiled rope from the front of your harness. The difference in the two performances will be dramatic and should cause you to think very carefully about the weight of equipment carried. The decision about how big a rack to carry must be based on the needs of safety and security on a particular route balanced with the need to keep weight down. Having 'non-dedicated' equipment is a help – krabs can be used as descendeurs as well as connectors, whereas a figure of eight descendeur is 'dedicated' to one purpose only.

As a very rough guide an average (30 m) pitch might require 10 or 12 pieces of pro-tection; if you know beforehand what form that protection takes your rack can be quite small and light. The harder and longer the pitch and the less you know, the more equipment you will carry.

## U.I.A.A. standards

U.I.A.A. standards are internationally recognised and approved safety standards for various items of equipment. Buying U.I.A.A. standard equipment ensures that what you buy is suitable and as safe as is practically possible for the function it is designed to perform. The standard itself, however, does not take into account the need, for instance, for gear that is ultra-light or totally non-restrictive. For these reasons the U.I.A.A. standard equipment may not always be the climber's preferred choice – though perhaps the best answer is to choose the U.I.A.A. standard equipment that best fulfils your extra criteria.

## Initial gear list for beginners

Helmet
Boots
Harness
Belay plate and screwgate krab

To share:
45 m × 11 mm rope
2 double tapes
4 short tapes
8 nuts
2 screwgate krabs
16 snaplink krabs

# 5  Ropecraft

Good rope techniques are obviously vital to the climber's safety, yet it is this area of climbing technique that one most often sees done badly. It is also the area of technique that beginners cannot afford to 'learn as they go along'. Perfect but basic ropework must be practised meticulously by all who use ropes in climbing. It is also better for a leader to know that his partner cannot handle ropes properly than not know and be lulled into a false sense of security. A climber should know his ropework thoroughly and be certain his techniques are absolutely correct. Many climbers survive for years thinking their ropework is immaculate until one day . . .

There are several component skills to good ropework that can easily be learnt before one starts belaying and anchoring for real. Before we look at these skills, however, it is worth setting out two key principles of safe ropework:

1  All the simple components of basic ropework *matter*; there is no room for even the slightest error in the practice of these techniques.

2  Once the ground has been left both members of a climbing pair should *either* be anchored *or* be belayed by the other.

## KNOTS

There are five basic knots to learn, and although one could get by with less, it is best to learn all five and have the choice of using the best knot to suit a particular situation. All knots reduce the strength of the rope, but some less than others. The amount of strength loss is due in part to the degree of bending the rope undergoes in the knot and in part the characteristics of the knot itself. The knots chosen here are therefore not the only suitable knots for any given situation, but they tend to be the strongest.

*The bowline*

## The bowline

*Use*　The basic knot for tying the climbing rope around one's waist (in the absence of a harness) or on to a harness.

*Comments*　Once tied, all the ropes that feed into the knot are fixed and cannot slide so there is no risk of the rope tightening around the waist. Because nylon rope is rather stiff and smooth it is essential to tie off the loose end of the bowline with a thumb knot to prevent the bowline working loose. The rope should be fairly tight around the waist to prevent it slipping up around the chest if the

*The bowline with thumb knot to prevent loosening*

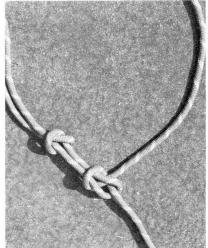

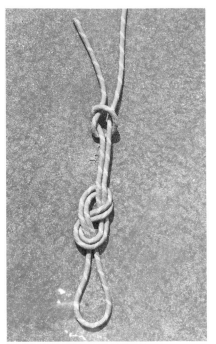

knot should be tied neatly and have a longish loose end (35 cm) to minimise the risk of the knot working loose. The knot is stronger if the loose end is on the inside of the first bend as it enters the knot. The loose end may be finished off with a thumb knot.

The figure of eight is a very fast knot to tie when a loop is required in a rope and it is relatively easy to untie when the rope is loaded.

*The bowline in use as the main rope attachment to the harness*

*A figure of eight knot tied on the bight and with a thumb knot to finish*

### Double fisherman's knot

*Use*    Joining two ropes together in emergency situations or for making rope slings.

*Comments*    A fairly difficult knot to tie and quite bulky when tied – good for the emergency situation but not needed for slings if ready-sewn tape slings are used. The strongest knot for joining two ropes. If used for making rope slings the loose ends should be taped to the sling to prevent the knot working loose.

climber is hanging on it. Ideally it should be possible to push your fingers down between rope and waist, but not your hands. The knot needs to be pulled tight, especially in stiff rope, as a loose knot can 'capsize' and turn itself into a slip knot.

of rope, and is therefore properly called a 'figure of eight on the bight'. If used to connect the rope directly to the harness it is difficult to tie and adjust but is less likely than the bowline to work loose or be inadvertently tied wrongly. The

*A double fisherman's knot*

### Figure of eight

*Use*    For connecting the climbing rope to harness, harness krab or anchor krab and used in anchoring the belayer.

*Comments*    In climbing always tied double, i.e. in a double piece

*A tape knot*

## Tape knot

*Use*   The only knot that can be used to form tape slings.

*Comments*   A simple knot to tie but one that needs regular and careful inspection if left permanently in a tape sling. This knot has a reputation for working loose or 'travelling'; tape is slippery material and knots in it tend to loosen easily. Check regularly that the knot is tight and that the loose ends are long enough (at least 8 cm). Some climbers are in the habit of taping the loose ends down, or even lightly sewing them to the main part of the tape; this practice has led to several accidents where the knot has worked loose but not become undone because of the taping or sewing. The knot then easily 'travels' along the tape until it is tied on a single strand of tape alone, the loop being held intact by a few stitches or insulation tape alone. If you want to make the knot safe it must be stitched through the knot itself, which is difficult to do; better still, buy ready stitched tapes.

*Tying a clove hitch*

## Clove hitch

*Use*   An increasingly popular knot for securing the belayer to a krab attached to an anchor. Invariably tied in the main rope and on to a krab.

*Comments*   An easy knot to tie, and very compact in use. Can be adjusted easily and is very fast to tie. It is not as strong as the alternative knot, the figure of eight, but a certain amount of slippage in the knot when loaded gives it a dynamic quality which should compensate for its lower absolute strength. It should always be tied to a screwgate krab as the knot twists under load and may then come into contact with the gate of a karabiner.

*The clove hitch*

## COILING AND UNCOILING THE ROPE

All the tangles and harassing delays we get in climbing are usually caused at the coiling or uncoiling stage. A rope can be coiled in the hand or around the neck; either way the coils should

*Coiling a rope: the coils ready for whipping*

hang neatly and be the correct length to be carried across the shoulder. Leave one loop uncoiled and fold back 30 cm of the other end. Then wrap the long end around the coils, working towards the folded end of rope. When the spare rope is nearly used up, feed the end through the loop formed by the folded end, pull tight and lock in place by pulling on the loose end of the folded portion of rope.

To uncoil, the whipping is undone in reverse order and the first coil thrown on to the floor with the end pulled out sideways so that it can be found later. Then the coils

are cast off one by one into an untidy heap. This ensures that individual coils do not fall through each other as they could if laid down neatly. The leader then ties on to the top end of the rope and the second to the end sticking out from the bottom of the pile.

A kinked rope should be hung over the crag and shaken so that the kinks untwist from the rope, then great care should be taken when coiling that the kinks are not being put back into the rope. A rope can kink by being pulled over a sharp edge with a load on it, or by being twisted as it is coiled.

*Whip the long end around a bight formed in the short end*

*Finishing off the whipping*

*A thread anchor suitable for an upward pull*

In waist belaying the belayer faces outwards with the ropes from harness to anchor passing around one side of the body. The slack is then taken in and the live rope put around the waist by dropping it over the head. It is very important that the live rope is on the same side of the body as the anchor ropes, thus counteracting any spinning action on the belayer during the holding of a fall. The rope on the dead side is wrapped once around the wrist of the dead hand to increase holding power. Long sleeves and leather gloves are advisable for the dead side at least. Clothing should also cover the waist as this area can be quite painful during the arrest of a fall. A good, stable and secure stance is particularly important when using a waist belay.

## THE ROPE IN LEADING

As we have already seen, leader and second are tied together at either end of the rope before climbing starts. In most circumstances the second must then anchor himself to the cliff or ground in some way so that he is held in position should he have to hold a falling leader. If the leader has put runners in the pitch then the second is in danger of being pulled upwards if the leader falls; he should therefore have anchors that prevent him being pulled upwards as well as downwards. If

the ground is steep below the crag then a falling leader with no runners could easily pull the second down the hillside if he has not anchored himself. If, however, the ground is flat below the crag and the leader is lighter than the second, or is unlikely to fall very far, or is unlikely to put any runners on the pitch, then seconds are frequently seen unanchored. This

is not to be recommended, however, as there is still the possibility of the second being pulled off balance or up in the air. Better to anchor always.

The leader climbs and the second's duty is to pay out the rope free from kinks, never causing the leader to drag the rope from him nor on the other hand ever allowing too much slack rope

*Leader and attentive second: Ron Fawcett on Elder Crack, Curbar Edge, in the Peak District*

*Tying on to a Whillans Harness: anchoring is achieved by tying back into the loop formed by the bowline, **not** into the krab*

to the harness and tied into the harness or harness belay loop with a figure of eight knot on the bight. The slack in the system is then taken up by moving back to the stance. Again the anchor ropes should be tight.

3   In some situations it is possible to clip the anchor krab directly into the belay loops on the harness, or to extend the anchor with a sling and again clip directly to the harness.

Note that a figure of eight on the bight may be used instead of the clove hitch in method 1, or that a clove hitch may be used instead of the figure of eight in method 2. When using multiple anchors these methods may be combined.

## Tying on to multiple anchors

The principle here is to equalise the load on all anchor points using combinations of the methods suggested in tying to a single anchor. A typical solution might be to clip directly to the harness with anchor no.1, then use the main rope with a clove hitch to anchor no.2. The clove hitch can then be adjusted to equalise the tensions on both anchors. Another commonly used method is to clip the rope through the krab on anchor no.1, bring it back to the harness and tie off with a figure of eight on the bight. The process is then repeated exactly for anchor no.2 and so on.

*Multiple anchors utilising a clove hitch and tape clipped direct to the harness central loop*

## STANCES

Stances are for the most part determined by the nature of the cliff and one's surroundings; one must make the best of what is on offer. Ideally a stance should be a flat ledge big enough for two with the anchors a short distance away and above and behind the belayer. The belayer should stand or sit facing outwards or sometimes sideways. Whatever the position, the belayer should feel stable and safe from being toppled by sudden loads.

Although it is an advantage to be able to see the second man climbing up, the leader should avoid lengths of rope between himself and the belay; these make him unstable as the rope will stretch. Ideally the belay ropes and the active rope to the climber below should be in a straight line so that any sudden pull on the belayer will not pull him out of position or cause his legs to collapse. If the ideal position is not possible then the belayer should sit down for greater stability and comfort.

## BELAYING

Belaying is the process of holding, paying out and taking in the rope for the person climbing. It is normally achieved by using a belay plate, but the waist belay method is also described here as it is still in quite common use and requires no specialist equipment. It must be said, however, that the belay plate or Italian hitch methods of belaying are far superior to the waist belay in terms of safety.

Before the rope is threaded through the belay plate the slack rope between belayer and climber is taken up. When the slack is gone a bight is made in the climbing rope and pushed through the belay plate. The bight is then clipped into a screwgate krab which is in turn clipped to the harness belay loop. If the belay plate has a thin cord attached to it this should be clipped to the same krab. Some belay plates have a spring to prevent inadvertent locking; this should be positioned between the plate and the krab. In certain situations one may wish to clip the belay plate direct to the anchor, thus transmitting any shock load direct to the anchor. This could be useful if a load on the belayer would be very uncomfortable, say on hanging ledgeless stances, or if the load were likely to topple the belayer. It should be stressed, however, that direct loading of the anchor (called a 'direct belay') requires an excellent, strong, 'bomb proof' anchor, and that it should always be possible to lock the belay plate.

Once threaded, the belayer is ready and the other person may climb. The 'live' rope leads to the climber, while the pile of spare rope on the floor is the 'dead' rope.

It is important to remember that in all belaying methods it is the hand on the 'dead' side that holds the rope after a fall, i.e. after the live rope has passed through the belay device or around the waist. Of vital importance therefore is the requirement that during belaying the dead side hand should never let go of the rope, even for a split second. If a leader falls during such a lapse then it is virtually impossible to regain control of the rope. The dead side hand, therefore, is moved along the rope by sliding rather than letting go and gripping again.

Falling climbers, especially leaders, acquire a tremendous amount of energy during a fall — the longer the fall, the greater the kinetic energy. This energy must be dissipated in halting the falling climber. The ground does it by using the kinetic energy to dig a large crater, but 'cratering' is a terminal option and to be avoided. Kinetic energy is absorbed in a number of ways: friction caused by the rope bending through protection krabs and by contact with the rock; the tightening of slack in all the components of the belay chain, especially knots; and the stretch in the rope itself is of course very important. If the resultant force on the belayer or his belay device is below a certain level then the device acts statically and stops the rope there and then — the faller at the other end is thus halted. Above a certain level the force causes the rope to run

*The Sticht plate in use – note that the 'dead side' hand (right hand in this case) must be clear of the rock*

through the belay device, creating heat by friction and thus dissipating the kinetic energy. The device is therefore acting 'dynamically'. Only a short amount of rope should run before the faller is halted.

Because of this feature of energy absorption by belay plates, the 'dead' (holding) hand should be held well clear of the plate and not gripped hard until the hand is pulled fully back to lock the device – even then the rope may run a little. Care should be taken to prevent the dead hand being pulled up against the plate as the belayer is then likely to let go. A second karabiner may be doubled up with the first one to create extra friction at the belay plate – this is recommended when the rope is used to protect a leader, especially

if the rope is thin, supple or slippery.

The braking action on a belay plate or Italian hitch is initiated by pulling the dead hand back to form an 'S' shape in the rope as it passes through the device. Great care must be taken therefore that there is sufficient space on the stance for the dead hand to be pulled back – ask yourself what will happen after a sudden loading; will your position on the stance change so that you are pressed against the cliff face and thus prevented from pulling back the dead hand?

The Italian hitch is used in the same way as the belay plate. It requires a large or pear-shaped screwgate krab to accommodate the hitch and cannot be used effectively with double rope climbing systems (see chapter 10).

*Braking with a Sticht plate*

## Waist belays

Waist belays are little used these days, but may be needed from time to time. They put great stress on the belayer during the arrest of a fall and are less likely to be successful, especially with beginners.

*A traditional waist belay. Note that the rope runs above the anchor rope and the belayer wears a glove on the 'holding' hand*

Anchors themselves will be dealt with in chapter 6; here we are concerned with how the climber fastens himself to the anchor. It should be remembered that the anchor itself is the only bit of the safety chain about which you may not be sure, involving as it does some contact with the natural environment of tree and rock. For that reason it is good practice always to use more than one anchor so that if one fails a back-

*Belaying from a single anchor point with a clove hitch*

up is always there. Blocks and spikes that appeared solid to experienced climbers have in the past come away from the rock with disastrous results. More than one anchor would have avoided the disasters in these cases.

Anchors for a downward pull should ideally be above the belayer and about a metre apart to stabilise the belayed climber. If the only belays available are low down then the belayer should sit down on the stance. A third anchor point, normally low, is required if an upward pull is likely, though some high anchors such as pitons, bolts or threads will suffice for both downward and upward pulls.

The belayer ties himself to the anchor points in such a way that any load on the anchors is shared equally amongst them. A belayer on flat ground at the foot of a climb needs only one anchor suitable for restraining an upward pull.

### Tying to a single anchor

Tying on can be achieved in any one of three ways:

1   Stand or sit in the position you wish to occupy when belaying, and estimate the distance between your harness 'tie in' and the anchor krab. Tie a clove hitch in the main rope at this estimated distance from your harness (or rather less to allow for bits of slack in the system), clip the clove hitch into the anchor krab and return to your stance. There should be no slack in the rope between you and the anchor; if there is then adjust the clove hitch by sliding rope through the slackened knot − no need to untie it.

2   Stand or sit at the stance, move twenty or thirty centimetres closer to the anchor and clip the main rope through the krab. The rope is then brought back

*Anchoring to a single point using a figure of eight on the bight*

between himself and the leader. The second feeds the rope through a belay device in normal belaying fashion. The leader fixes running belays, clipping them to the rope with a karabiner. If he falls one metre above his last running belay then he will probably fall about three metres. This three metres is comprised of the two metres he would fall because he was a metre above his last runner, plus another metre because all the slack bits in the belay system are tightened and because the rope stretches in a fall. The leader now has the choice of regaining the rock and trying again or being lowered to the ground by the second. Assuming no mishaps, falls are quite rare; the leader reaches the stance at the top of the pitch, finds two or three suitable anchors and belays himself in preparation for the second man following.

## CLIMBING CALLS

Communication between climbers can be amazingly difficult on lots of rock climbs. Long pitches, rock bulges, wind and convex slopes all make communication difficult or even impossible. Two experienced climbers well used to each other's methods can climb quite safely and successfully without the need to call to each other, but for everyone else a simple and standardised system of calls is

required. Calls must be short, simple and distinctive; complicated calls with lots of syllables become jumbled and incoherent in the wind and can be misunderstood with unfortunate results.

There are two commonly used systems of calls; use either but not both. The second, American, system is rather simpler and more functional:

*Taking in*　The call by the leader to indicate he is taking up the slack rope hand over hand – *NOT* a signal for the second to unfasten his belay.

*That's me*　The response from the second when all the slack is taken in; it lets the leader know there are no snags or jammed rope between him and the second. On hearing this call the leader should put the rope into a belay plate and belay the second.

*Climb when you're ready* The leader says this when fully prepared in belay position. The second now unfastens his belays.

*Climbing*　Second calls to leader.

*OK*　The leader's response; the second begins to climb.

'Take in' and 'slack' are two calls the climber could use on the climb. An urgent cry of 'tight rope!' is also often heard, but all these commands are self-explanatory.

More experienced climbers quite effectively miss out the 'climb when you're ready' and 'climbing' calls and so simplify the system further. If the leader immediately begins to belay when he hears 'that's me', then the second can unfasten his belay and begin to climb on the leader's reply of 'OK'.

The other standard system is as follows:

*On belay*　Belayer to climber: the belayer is now ready to protect the climber.

*Climb*　Belayer to climber: an instruction to the climber to climb, but can be omitted as 'on belay' means the same thing.

*Climbing*　The climber shouts to the belayer.

*Off belay*　Said by either party, this means that the caller is anchored and therefore no longer needs to be belayed.

## THE ART OF BELAYING

We have looked at the mechanics of belaying and conditions necessary for safe belaying but there is more to it than that. A belayer is part of a team and has a role in that team of inspiring confidence in the climber and also enabling the climber to get the best out of himself by slick belay work.

Apart from belaying properly in the ways already described the belayer can help the climber, mainly by being attentive. The art is to keep the rope 'exactly right' as far as the climber is concerned; it must feed out when the leader moves up, but slack must be taken in when he steps down again, and by just the right amount. Forty centimetres too much slack and you increase the potential length of fall by a metre; too tight and you cause the leader to work harder or even pull him off. No leader is helped psychologically if he looks down and sees a great loop of slack at the belayer's feet. All slack must be taken in without the rope becoming tight. The same applies to the belayer bringing up a second person; the rope is not there to pull up that person, but at the same time it should respond immediately to the second moving up. The belayer should gently feel the movements of the climber transmitted through the rope.

Careful attention to detail inspires confidence and therefore maximises performance potential.

### The safety chain

The notion of a 'safety chain' is a theme that should be applied to all ropecraft in climbing, right through from anchoring to leading. The safety chain rule tells us that all links in the chain should be of equal strength. Any link that is substantially weaker means that the whole chain is weak and that the 'strong' links are being wasted. Similarly it is pointless, for instance, carrying a super heavy, super strong sling for an anchor if one clips on to the sling with a 2000 kg krab. To save weight, then, all links in a chain from anchor to belayer to leader should be of equal strength. To complicate this simple rule, however, it should be noted that different parts of a system may not be loaded equally; an anchor krab may experience little load compared to a leader's tie-in krab if the leader falls, because there are lots of bends and points of friction in the rope before load is transmitted back to the anchor.

# 6 Anchors

The ability to select good solid anchor points is obviously a very important aspect of climbing technique. A certain amount of technical 'know-how', a quick eye for a suitable belay point and lots of experience in anchor selection are the combined skills needed to cover this aspect effectively.

*A spike anchor in use as a running belay*

Although we are looking here at anchors for the belayer on a stance, all the techniques apply to the leader looking for running belays, except perhaps that the leader may be glad of a poor running belay whereas the belayer must always be sure he has good anchors. Natural belays will be dealt with first; these are belays utilising natural rock features or trees. Artificial anchors such as pitons, nuts and bolts, are considered second.

## SPIKES

Spikes are the most common natural belay to be found on most crags, though some types of rock are notably devoid of good spike belays. They can range in size and shape from tiny sharp flakes a few centimetres across to huge pinnacle-like spikes a few metres high and wide. Whatever their size they should all be inspected for safety and stability in approximately the same way. The inspection goes something like this:

*Is it safe?*
Check by banging with the fist or kicking; any dull hollow sound,

movement or vibration indicates a doubtful anchor point. Look at the base of the flake for possible fracture lines splitting it from the main body of rock; avoid if these are present.

*Will the sling stop in place?*
Spikes with rounded tops combined with a pull from the side may result in the sling rolling off. Tape slings may stop in place more readily. If the space behind the spike or flake is too restricted for a rope sling then a tape will usually fit. Make sure the sling is plenty long enough to sit comfortably around the spike and that the sling and krab are loaded in a mechanically sound manner. This means that the sling sides must form a narrow 'V' at the krab. A wide 'V' is loading the sling too greatly and may break it. The krab must also be loaded so that the sling loads one end and the climbing rope the other. A krab loaded across the sides or gate is very weak.

*Are there any sharp edges?*
Flakes and spikes with sharp edges where the tape is touching them should be avoided. Thick tape slings should be used where the edges are anything like sharp and unavoidable.

Slings on spikes used for running belays have a habit of lifting off after the climber has passed unless the spike is exactly along the run of the rope. Pulls to one side will result in the sling lifting off as the climber moves. Lengthen the sling by attaching another one to avoid dragging the climbing rope out of line. Tape slings are less liable to fall off than rope slings.

## BLOCKS

Blocks are similar to spikes in most respects. They are usually found lying on ledges or at the bottom and tops of crags. They are detached from the main bulk of rock but may be heavy or well embedded enough to hold a fall. They should be tested in the same way as a spike. If they are too large for a sling to fit then the main rope can be looped over them and tied back into the harness normally. Frequently two or more blocks are jammed together and their points of contact sometimes form thread belays. Be wary in such a situation that a load cannot prise the two blocks away from each other.

## THREAD BELAYS

Threads are found occurring naturally as water or wind-worn eyeholes in the rock through which

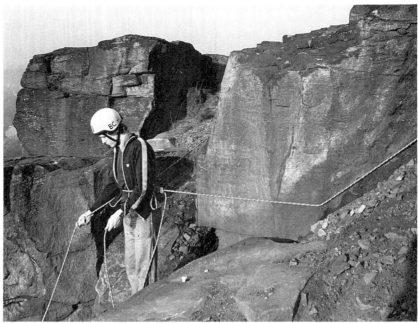

*Tying on to a very large block using the main rope and a figure of eight knot to tie the anchor rope back into the waist*

*A thread belay formed by two blocks touching*

a sling can be threaded. Alternatively, a crack may close at one point or a chockstone may be jammed in it, both enabling a sling to be threaded around the obstruction. The two ends of the sling are clipped together with a krab after threading. Thread belays are very useful in that they work for upward as well as downward pulls, essential when belaying a leader who has placed running belays. Chockstones and jammed blocks may not be good for an upward pull; check that they will not pull out or lever apart in that situation. Tape slings may pull out through very small gaps around chockstones; rope slings may be better here. Arrange slings around chockstones so that the sides of the sling sit down opposite sides of the chockstone. Also twist one end of the sling before joining with a krab to ensure that if part of it pulls through one side of the chockstone the krab will not drop off the sling.

It is impossible to thread many tiny holes with a tape sling; a useful alternative is to thread the wire on a wire nut through the hole. Once threaded the nut can be pushed down the wire somewhat leaving two wire loops to be connected by a krab. The wire can also be 'pre-bent' to aid threading.

## TREES

Low-lying crags frequently have trees growing on ledges or out of cracks and chimneys. Trees growing on crags are usually of a fairly tenacious variety; they must be to grow from tiny cracks in otherwise solid rock. They do therefore make good anchors if they are thick enough and still alive. A tree 8 cm in diameter is probably the minimum trunk size that would suffice for a main belay anchor. Check that the roots are sound by pushing the tree; if the earth around the base is lifted then it is most likely unsafe. Put a sling around the tree, joined with a krab, and make sure it stops as close to the base of the trunk as possible to avoid any unnecessary leverage.

Some types of conifer should be avoided when small as they have very shallow root systems and are very easily uprooted.

## PITONS

(Usually called pegs or pins)

If there is no good natural anchor then a piton or nut must be used. Pitons will be dealt with first, but if at all possible nuts should be used in preference to pitons mainly because of the rock damage done by repeated hammering of pitons.

Pitons are of two main types; those made of soft steel and those made from hard chrome molybdenum steel. Both types have their advantages, but in most situations hard steel pitons are safer and of more use. On rock such as limestone, however, where the cracks and holes are twisted and the rock is hard and brittle, soft steel pitons are usually placed more easily and to greater effect. They are, however, more difficult to remove and consequently once placed they are frequently left in place for future parties – a practice which avoids rock damage but can leave dubious and in time rusted pitons for those following.

Pegs come in five main styles, each type being best fitted for one or two situations.

*Horizontal pitons* These are most common, consisting of a metal

*A horizontal blade peg*

blade with the eye at right-angles. Used in narrow horizontal and vertical cracks.

*Angle* A folded length of sheet metal for wider cracks, U or V-shaped, and potentially dangerous if inserted the wrong way. Fits cracks from 1 cm to 5 cm.

*Bong* A large-angle piton for cracks up to 15 cm wide. The body of the piton usually has holes drilled to lighten it.

*Leeper* A piton with a Z-shape, used in similar situations to the angle, but has great holding power if inserted correctly.

*Knife blade and rurp* Pegs with very thin blades for tiny cracks. Not normally used for belaying. The

*Ron Fawcett on the scary wall climbing of Space Babble, Yosemite Valley*

*John Stevenson climbing at Freyr,
Ardennes, Belgium*

9    *Laybacking on Zeus, Burbage Edge,
Peak District*

*An angle peg in a vertical crack*

rurp is the smallest piton available, used for direct aid only and never for belays.

## Placement of pitons

Always look for a piton placement that gives the best mechanical advantage to the piton. Imagine a nail being placed loosely in the crack or hole; will it stop there without dropping out; does the shape of the crack such as widening or constriction hold it in place; does the crack slope downwards into the rock so that the nail's weight holds it there? If the answers are 'yes', then you have a good place for a peg. Other cracks will do, but will not be as good. Select a peg of a size that

will fit just over half-way into the crack without hammering, then two or three good hammer blows should drive the eye in to almost touch the rock. A musical ringing noise increasing in pitch as the peg is driven home indicates a good piton. When fully driven in, bounce the hammer on the piton head; it should bounce back and not move the piton.

Individual types require special treatment. An angle piton should be placed in horizontal cracks with the head downwards, the two ends of the inverted V-shape biting into the bottom face of the crack. Leepers should be placed in vertical cracks with the eye flange uppermost so that a load compresses the Z-shape and causes it to bite further into the

crack sides. A leeper should have its eye down in a horizontal crack.

If you do not have a peg to fit the crack size then you have two choices: either select the next size up and drive it in as far as possible or stack two pitons together and insert them as one. Neither method is advisable for main belays, but the techniques are frequently used for aid climbing (using pitons or other devices for directly aided ascent) or running belays. Leepers make the best stacked pitons, or a leeper and an angle; others are less suitable. If a peg can only be part driven then it should be tied off in some way. This means that a sling is fastened to the body of the peg where it touches the rock so that any load does not put a large leverage force

*A protruding angle peg 'tied off'*

*A 'tied-off' peg with back-up*

on the eye. The problem is that most hard steel pegs have fairly sharp edges or are made of thin sheet metal and this tends to cut tape or thin rope when loaded on the peg. A 20 mm tape can break on a sharp peg after a fall of only half a metre. Perhaps the best method is to tie off the peg with the thickest rope sling that will stop in place, using a clove hitch to fasten it. A back-up sling can be attached to the eye of the peg with a krab so that it hangs loosely between the eye and the krab on the 'tie-off'.

### Removing pitons

Hit the peg backwards and forwards a couple of times, aiming for the thickest part of the eye. This should loosen the peg so that it can be pulled out with the fingers. Angles need only be hit sideways a fraction of an inch, creating a groove and enabling them to slide out. After having placed and removed a few pitons, or seen the effects of an aid climb up a crack in soft rock, you will realise what a mess pegs can make of the rock. Each successive placement in a fairly hard rock like granite will change the size of the hole and so alter the rock. Many knife-blade cracks have now got holes large enough for a hand jam. Nuts do not have this effect, and if they are well placed in a good crack they are probably much safer than the usual rusted-in-place piton with unknown holding power.

## NUTS

Most nuts, even more than pitons, require a crack that is shaped to fit them. A gradually narrowing crack, a widening or an obstruction in the crack are all elements to look for in placing a nut. Unlike pitons, nuts will usually lift out if pulled in a particular direction so that the anticipated direction of pull must be borne in mind when selecting a placement. Cracks which are narrow at the entrance make excellent main belay nut placements as the pull

*A typical nut placement in a narrowing crack*

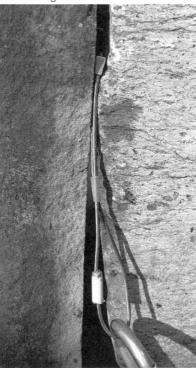

can come from almost any angle. A nut for an upward pull may, in many cases, have to be used in conjunction with the normal downward pull belays. Hexagonal nuts can be used to great effect in horizontal but parallel-sided cracks and even in vertical ones, but they must be a good tight fit and they are less reliable for main belays than conventionally placed nuts. Remember that whatever is used for a main belay needs to be fairly strong, so wedges on thin rope (less than 5 mm) or the thinnest wired wedges should be avoided for this purpose. Wired nuts in general are less suited to main belays than roped nuts because any movement of the belayer tends to move the wire, which may in turn work the nut loose. Avoid placing nuts between blocks or behind hollow-sounding flakes; the cracks may widen under load and allow the nut to pop out. Nuts frequently wedge in cracks because of tiny bumps or protrusions on the rock wall; such placements should be avoided as the protrusions may break off or pulverise under load.

Nowadays nuts are extremely important for the leader's belays and therefore nut placement is dealt with in greater depth in connection with leading in chapter 10.

Expanding cam devices will normally hold in the cracks not suitable for conventional nuts and may be used for running or main belays. Watch out for contact of all cams on the rock and freedom from a load that will bend the stem of solid-stemmed models.

## BOLTS

Putting bolts into rock climbs is an emotive issue. It has been accepted as the normal method of running belay provision in some climbing areas (particularly Western Europe), while in other countries bolts are used sparingly where nothing else will suffice, and even then only in certain areas, as is the case in the United States and U.K. Bolts are objected to on two main issues: first, that they remove variation in the boldness and adventurous qualities of routes by allowing regular placement of protection where there otherwise would be none, so that the route becomes predictably safe; and second, that bolts are a permanent and artificial addition to the rock and require destruction of the rock in placing them. The latter argument is perhaps a little spurious as 'bolt damage' is small compared to the effects of chalk, boot rubber, 'cleaning' routes and general climbing traffic.

Bolts for climbing, called drill anchors, sleeves or spitz, are normally hard steel 10 mm self-drilling expansion bolts. They require a hammer and driver to place – the driver is a heavy metal tube that fits over the end of the bolt during drilling to protect the bolt from the hammer. Bolts should be drilled in clean flat unfractured rock and should be mechanically sound in their positioning: that is, a load should not tend to pull the bolt outwards. Great care should be taken when drilling that the hole is not made too wide by sloppy drilling, or that the area around the mouth of the hole is not fractured. A depth marker on the sleeve indicates when the hole is deep enough; the sleeve is then extracted and fitted with a plug which expands the sleeve as the bolt is driven into the hole. When complete the bolt sleeve should be flush with the rock surface. A bolt and stainless steel bent plate hanger are then screwed into the sleeve (spanner or Allen key needed) and tightened gently. Under roofs a ring bolt would be better to avoid the twisting action of a normal hanger used in this situation.

It is worth bearing in mind that bolts, like pegs, that have been placed by someone else may not be sound, or may have become unsound. Fractured rock, wobbly bolts or heavily rusted pegs (especially on sea cliffs) are all danger signs.

## CONNECTING THE ANCHOR TO THE BELAYER

Generally the anchor sling, peg, bolt or nut is connected to the main rope with a krab and then the belayer ties on by fastening the main rope back into his harness with a figure of eight knot on a bight. The krab used should preferably be a screwgate type, especially if it is liable to contact rock as is likely when clipping into pegs. If the belayer needs to belay close to the anchor then the belay sling can be clipped directly into the belayer's harness using a screwgate krab with the gate downwards. Karabiner gates in all cases should face away from anything liable to contact them and so open the gate.

# 7 Climbing techniques 1

To watch young children climbing trees and scrambling around obstacles is a sight all climbers should experience regularly. They exhibit pure natural movement free of the inhibitions we develop as we age, not to mention the loss of flexibility normally experienced as we get older. Climbing techniques should not be stylised; they should be an attempt to return to natural movement that utilises the natural talents of the body type we possessed as young children. Then there are skills we can develop to aid that natural fluidity; a deep awareness of balance and distribution of our body weight is perhaps the most important of climbing skills. A gymnast develops these same skills, but his are an attempt to have perfect control of his weight distribution in formalised and known situations. In climbing, the next situation or body position is always unknown; it will be different from the last similar situation because the holds will be in a slightly different place or the rock will be more slippery than before. These situations require us to look at each move and judge what kind of move is required and how we balance or distribute our weight. This may seem quite natural to most climbers with some experience, but it is a development of this natural talent by being aware of the body that makes progress in rock climbing possible. This chapter contains much technical information on types of handholds and footholds and how best to use them, but this knowledge is unimportant compared to the advice on balance, weight distribution and movement on rock. Also remember that we all come in different shapes and sizes, and these characteristics determine what kind of movement we do best, which is usually the type we like best. Shortish muscular climbers usually like powering their way up fiercely overhanging cracks, lighter longer climbers may like intricate slabs and walls best, while ape-like climbers love swinging about on overhanging rock on big holds. It is correct to develop these talents while being conversant with the full range of climbing techniques, but it would be wrong to try and stylise ourselves into 'the standard climber'.

All the techniques and movement forms mentioned here can be practised on boulders and low bits of crag where you can jump off happily. Indeed, bouldering is the ideal place to perfect these movement abilities or regain lost flexibility. Being a perfect boulderer is not necessarily the same as being an excellent rock climber, however; the climber is one who has sufficient control and confidence in his movement abilities to perform them in the much more exposed situation high on a rock face.

## HANDHOLDS AND FOOTHOLDS

Movement on rock is achieved by use of a combination of hand and footholds; without them that particular piece of work would be impossible. The beginner often sees climbers ascending what appears to be a holdless sheet of rock; it will certainly not be, but the skilled climber has learned to see holds where the beginner sees nothing. This perhaps is the most fundamental skill in the use of holds for climbing – the art of seeing, recognising and anticipating where holds will be found. A hold can be described as literally any blemish on the rock that breaks its smoothness, the slightest wrinkle or scoop is a hold to the experienced climber. The beginner looks for more obvious features such as ledges, flat holds or spikes first, but with growing experience recognises the subtler features on the rock that form the finger holds, smear holds or side holds. Different types of rock have different kinds of holds; knowing the characteristic of a particular rock helps the climber anticipate the location and type of the holds. Limestone, for instance, is covered in a profusion of small, sharp holds and pockets forming excellent finger and handholds, but poor for the feet. Gritstone in contrast has few holds but the rock is broken into large blocks bordered by vertical and horizontal cracks, usually with rounded edges

requiring expertise in jamming techniques. Seeing the climb from below and knowing the type of rock, the climber can usually form a good idea of the kind of holds and type of climbing which are to be met on the route.

The individual types of holds are described below. Most are described and named as handholds, but remember that any handhold can also be used for the feet as well. Holds are in fact for any part of the body, but they work better with some parts than others.

*Jugs and incuts*    These are the big inward-sloping holds that your hands or fingers curl over and grip securely. Jugs are large incuts; smaller ones are perhaps just big enough for one joint of the fingers but they still feel secure and are the best kind of hold to have. A great deal of height can be made on an incut hold because hands or fingers are unlikely to slip off even when the body is high and therefore pulling outwards on the hold. Incuts are sometimes just slots in the rock, especially on limestone, and this makes them difficult to use as a foothold.

*Flat holds*    or small ledges make good holds for the hands from below, but care must be taken when attempting to move high on the hold as friction preventing the hand sliding off outwards is limited. Flat holds do, however, make excellent footholds, frequently allowing the whole foot to be

*Although a poor handhold, this rounded flat hold makes an excellent foothold*

placed on the hold and so resting the leg muscles. On larger flat holds, i.e. ledges, and sometimes on small ones, a technique known as 'the mantelshelf' is employed to gain maximum height from one hold. The mantelshelf (or 'mantel') consists of a pulling stage when the body is pulled upwards on the hold fairly quickly, and while momentum is maintained the hands (or hand) are turned into a pushing upwards position on the hold until body weight is balanced on straightened arms above the hold. Then a foot is placed on the hold and the climber stands up, helped by any handholds on the wall above.

*Sloping holds*    are the poorest form of hand or finger hold, offering little friction to the hand to pull up with. It is usually best to feel

A mantelshelf sequence: (a) the climber prepares to spring; (b) a quick

spring gets the weight balanced over the hands; (c) one foot is brought up to

the same ledge and one hand seeks a higher hold

A large sloping hold improved by finding wrinkles that stop the fingers slipping

*A pressure hold – a downward push with palm inwards*

*Using a finger hold*

*Small footholds are best used with the front inside edge of the boot*

*A sidehold being used to pull the body weight over onto the right foot*

around a sloping hold for the best position to grip the hold; sometimes a little bump or hollow will make the hold more usable. Although little use from below, the sloping hold can be quite useful from above as a foothold or pushing hold for the hand. Pushing or pressure holds are used by turning the palm inwards and the fingers downwards and pushing up or sideways on the hold to enable a reach to be made with the other hand or a balanced position to be gained with the feet.

*Small holds*   require specialised techniques if they are to be useful. They can be used to maintain balance or even pull up on during difficult climbs. Finger-tip holds are best used by straightening the last two sections of the fingers, knuckles pointing upwards and forearms close to the rock. This enables maximum power to be used on quite small holds. Small holds can make excellent

footholds if the climber's footwear is stiff enough. The section of boot between the big toe and the ball of the foot is best used for small holds, although with Vibram-soled mountain boots the toe of the boot can be used quite effectively. Despite all the advice to the contrary in other parts of this chapter, the best way to ensure that feet stay on poor or small footholds is to lean out away from the rock so that the body weight pushes the feet into the rock as well as downwards. Of course good handholds are essential for this to be done effectively.

*Side holds*   are most useful on wall climbs where a lot of the moves involve stepping up sideways to a foothold. In these situations a side hold for the hand is more useful than a horizontal hold; the body weight is being rocked over the foot with a sideways pull. Side holds occur as frequently as other holds; look for them in rock with vertical lines such as ribs and cracks. One edge of a crack makes an excellent side hold.

*Undercuts* are like upside-down incut holds and are usually found beneath little overhangs, overlaps or downward-hanging flakes. They are rarely useful to pull up with, but once the climber is high enough to be able to pull outwards on the undercuts they become excellent holds, feeling more secure the higher one moves. Undercuts beneath flakes make excellent holds but are sometimes insecure. Check well before using, as a great outward force is put on an undercut in use.

An undercut hold

A pinch grip

Feet smearing where there are no definite footholds

*Smear holds* are essentially footholds that are so sloping that the foot only stays in place by friction. On a slab that is too steep for walking up relying on friction, the climber looks for slight scoops and depressions in the rock where the angle is slightly less. Such places make ideal smear holds. Usually with rock boots, the boot is placed carefully on the hold, toes pointing uphill and heels dropped down low. Body weight is then carefully balanced over the smeared foot and the next move made. Smearing is virtually impossible wearing stiff Vibram-soled mountain boots; the climber must look for tiny edges for his boots in this case.

*Pinch grips* usually occur on tiny vertical ribs of rock, frequently between two cracks or on the edge of a flake. In essence they are like sideholds improved by a second opposing sidehold for the thumb. The two holds are gripped tightly like a pincer so that straight pulling-up moves can be made with them − a move impossible with a plain side hold.

*Cracks* are the obvious lines of weakness up a cliff face; to the experienced climber they offer the

A difficult crack climb: Elaine Brooks on Rixon's Pinnacle, (5.10) Yosemite Valley

surest continuous line of holds up that section of cliff. Cracks offer the possibility of a variety of holds on the crack itself and hidden away inside it. The majority of crack climbing involves jamming, a technique dealt with later, but cracks also offer sideholds on the edge or hidden inside the crack, jugs and undercuts inside where chockstones are jammed and excellent flat holds where vertical and horizontal cracks cross. A crack is a line of weakness in the rock so it is here that there are likely to be more features usable as holds.

## MOVING ON ROCK

Walking is the most common human balancing act − balancing on one foot, nearly overbalancing then catching the balance again on the other foot. Climbers use exactly the same principles when they move up rock; the action is just like climbing stairs. Balance is gained on the higher foot by pushing the body weight over that foot, then the lower foot can be brought through on to the stair above and the process repeated. Arms are used on the handrails only for steadying purposes. This kind of balancing movement is imitated as far as possible in climbing; this is easy on slabs and less steep walls but becomes less feasible on cracks, steep walls and chimneys, although the basic principles are still there.

*Difficult slab climbing with weight over the feet and a good view of the moves head: Jill Lawrence leads Maxine's Wall (5.10), Yosemite Valley*

Easier climbs are usually best accomplished by using this stair-climbing technique. Because the weight is nearly always over one foot or the other little work is done by the arms, which are of course weaker than legs when it comes to moving the body steeply upwards. This upright posture also means that the upper body is away from the rock, leaving the climber with a good view of his next footholds and the route ahead. Another important feature of this style is the way in which footholds are used: weight acting vertically downwards pushes the boot on to the foothold and helps keep it there. Leaning too close to the rock, as beginners tend to do, pushes the feet downwards parallel to the rock, so increasing the chances of them slipping off. Try it on a boulder some time and see the difference.

The young climber will soon graduate to steeper climbs, and although the principles are the same, the climb is not usually accomplished in the same manner as staircase climbing. The basis of harder, steeper climbing is still that the weight should be balanced over one foot or the other and transferred as the climber moves, but this can only be accomplished by moving in a 'side to side' kind of way with the body quite close to the rock. The idea is to keep the body close to the rock to preserve balance and strength, then move up by selecting a foothold to one side, putting the leg out sideways on to the hold, using a sidehold to 'rock' the body weight over the new foothold and finally pushing upwards on the foothold to gain height. In 'staircase' style climbing it is normal to have three points of contact with the rock at any one time, i.e. only one limb at a time is moved. This is fine on easy routes and for the careful, steady, but rhythmical movement aimed at in this style of climbing. Harder climbs are rarely best accomplished by always having three points of contact. 'Side to side' movements are frequently more rhythmical and fluid with two points of contact in movement situations, and three or four points in rest situations. The climber can move his body around much more flexibly and with a greater range of movement if less than three points of contact are used. On very difficult climbs, of course, there are rarely enough holds to enable more than two-point contact anyway, and the 'side to side' style must be used. So far both methods can be accomplished almost entirely on footwork; all the upward work is done by the legs with arms reserved for balance and side to side manoeuvring. In practice, however, the arms are frequently used for upward movement where the footholds are poor, in the wrong position or even non-existent. In this situation the climber tries to move fairly quickly and in one continuous movement until the next supporting foothold is reached and a balanced position achieved on it.

Moves, no matter how easy, must be planned ahead. The climber looks ahead for the next two or three moves, or until a definite resting spot can be seen, and plans out what kind of movements will be likely. A memory for moves is developed and on steeper rock a memory of foothold position must also be developed as the climber is usually too close to the rock to see them. Only experience will enable the climber to be able to look at a combination of holds and see what kind of movements are needed. If the climber always practises this,

trying to work out moves for himself, then this experience is soon gained. A climber's eventual style will be suited to his own body type and character, but by observing good climbers, certain similarities will always be noted. Smoothness, neatness, coolness

and a kind of flowing movement are all common characteristics of good climbers; it is the kind of style that makes difficult moves look easy, strenuous moves effortless, and scary positions are handled as though they were next to the ground.

*Sideholds and careful 'foot to foot' balancing movements are the key to progress on this steep wall: Pete Gomersall on the first ascent of Screech Owl (E3), Crafnant, North Wales*

# 8　Climbing techniques 2

Now we can look at the various specialised techniques needed to tackle certain rock features. Although the general principles of movement outlined previously still hold good, the techniques required for these specific rock features are not natural movements like climbing trees or stairs. Some form of specialised knowledge about the feature is required to climb successfully.

## SLABS

Slabs vary in steepness and smoothness from rock that is easy to walk up without hands to rock that needs positive holds rather than pure friction to enable an ascent to be made. Easy slabs can be walked up using feet alone; this is good practice as it ensures an upright posture with weight acting through the feet. A smooth continuous momentum, preferably in a direct uphill line rather than sideways, usually works best. Toes normally point straight up the line of ascent and the whole of the front half of the sole is in contact with the rock. Look for areas of slab that are slightly flatter than the other places, or pebbles stuck in the rock that help prevent the foot moving. If the slab gets steeper then hands must be used as well as feet. While the feet continue their smearing action the hands are used to press up on the rock almost like a second pair of feet. Fingers should point down the slab and the hands should be low down, fairly close to the feet ensuring that the climber's weight is still balanced over his points of contact. Short steps are usually better so that feet are kept all the time beneath the body weight with consequently less danger of slipping.

As the slab gets steeper still, friction alone will not be enough and any sort of hold, no matter how tiny, is sought to aid friction. Even fingernail-width holds may provide the extra 'uplift' to counteract a slowly sliding foot. Holds on slabs are rare, but can be used to the full; a hold is reached at full stretch, pulled up on, and with sufficient momentum the feet walk up the slab until one foot can be placed on the hold and a standing position attained. Small holds are used for the fingertips and inside edges of boots: a sharp-edged boot sole helps here, though it is amazing what improbable holds rock climbing boots will adhere to.

Slab climbing can be very enjoyable but also quite scary; slabs rarely have many places where running belays can be arranged and they are most difficult to reverse, i.e. climb back down, if required.

*Slab climbing using a combination of small finger holds, palming and smearing*

## WALLS

Wall climbing on steep rock demands little in the way of specialised technique other than the advice given on general movement on rock. A good economical 'weight over feet' and 'close to the rock' style is all that is required. Sideholds to aid a 'side to side' kind of movement and large footholds or ledges to rest on are the features to look out for on a wall climb. It is usually best to identify the line of holds and possible resting spots before climbing, because the 'close to the rock style' used in wall climbing makes it difficult to spot holds once embarked on the climb. Resting ledges or large footholds should be used to rest the arms for a minute or so; do this by dangling them down, one at a time if a handhold is still needed. This enables more blood to flow and so supply the muscles.

Even on quite steep walls it is possible to climb 'in balance', that is, climb using hands for steadying only rather than gripping tight to hold oneself in position. With this balanced style flat holds that are useless once they have been pulled up on can be used further by pushing down on to gain height on a foothold. A good practice is to find a foothold on a steepish boulder and try to balance the whole body weight on it without using the arms. The easiest way to do this is to stick the knee out sideways, leg fully bent, and sit your thigh on to your heel. The other leg just hangs down, perhaps pressing the rock for stability and acts as a counterbalance. From this position it is possible to gain height by using low handholds to push up on and aid the leg muscles in this movement. Wall climbing can be very strenuous despite an excellent technique. Fitness in the arms is obviously an asset for successful wall climbing.

## CHIMNEYS

Chimneys are cracks wide enough to climb up inside rather than outside. Of course they vary in width tremendously and so demand varying techniques dependent upon width. Whatever the size, the climber has to decide which way to face; usually feet go on the wall with most holds, back on the smoothest wall. It is also best, however, to have the back on the least steep wall of the chimney; sometimes it is necessary to try both ways to discover the easiest method. Very narrow chimneys are called squeeze chimneys and are very strenuous, progress being made by lots of small movements. With hands downwards pushing up on the opposite wall and legs slightly bent with feet jammed, a

*Steep wall climbing on pocketed limestone*

few inches of height can be gained. Then breathe in or turn the shoulders slightly to wedge so that the legs, feet and hands can be moved up to prepare for the next movement.

Slightly wider chimneys can be climbed sideways or with the arms pressing outwards on opposite walls as the legs are drawn up. Legs are then pressed outwards, enabling the arms and body to move up, and so on. This is a good fast method that only works in chimneys of about shoulder width.

Wider chimneys require the use of 'backing and footing' or 'straddling' techniques. To 'back and foot', back, arms and one foot are pressed on one wall with the other foot counteracting this pressure on the opposite wall. By pressing on the back wall with arms and foot the body can be raised, then the back pressed on the wall again to rest. Both feet are placed on the opposite wall and 'walked up' half a metre or so before regaining the original moving position. It is possible to rest quite comfortably with feet on one wall and back braced against the other.

Straddling a chimney is less strenuous, more stylish and faster, but it does require one or two holds on both walls. Hands push downwards and outwards against holds on opposite walls as the feet and body are moved up. Feet are then pressed out on to holds (the same holds the hands are on for a flexible person!) and the body and hands moved up. Of course, rock being so variable a combination of both methods is fairly common.

## CRACKS

Crack techniques and jamming are the most important single set of techniques to learn in rock climbing. Beginners invariably find

*Chimney technique on the Peapod (HVS), Curbar Edge, Peak District*

*Straddling a wide chimney*

jamming difficult and painful; but once learnt the techniques are nearly always used in preference to other more strenuous and less secure methods of climbing cracks. Jamming a crack is a very sure way of ascending a particular piece of rock; protection with nuts is usually good and the climbing feels secure with no problem about searching for the next hold. Overhanging walls are usually climbed by crack lines; cracks can turn a formidable proposition into a reasonable one.

Cracks, of course, vary in size from thin finger-tip lines to 20 cm wide fissures. Much wider and they become chimneys. Techniques can be conveniently divided into finger cracks; hand and fist cracks; off-width cracks; and laybacking, which can be practised on any size of crack.

*Finger cracks* are perhaps the most strenuous of jam cracks because weight is taken on the fingers with little chance of feet being jammed in the crack to take some of the weight. As with all jamming, the climber should look for a narrowing of the crack so that the hand or fingers can be put into the wider section above, then slid down and allowed to jam naturally in the narrowing. If no narrowing is present in finger cracks then the fingers are put into the crack and twisted with the hand. To do this it is invariably best to invert the hand before jamming so that the thumb points downwards. When twisting

*A long finger-jamming crack where excellent jams have been formed where earlier piton-aided ascents have widened the crack: Serenity Crack (5.11), Yosemite Valley*

*A finger jam*

occurs the first two (strongest) fingers tend to twist together and so widen and jam, then the fingers can be used to pull – usually painful. With or without natural jam placements in the crack, it is usually best to climb finger cracks with the hand inverted for the jam. Exceptions occur when a long stretch has to be made from a finger jam: then the lower jam is made with thumb uppermost and the upper hand is used with thumb downwards. Sometimes rugosities on the wall to the side of the crack can be pinch gripped by the thumb to aid the jam. Feet are an embarrassment in finger cracks; they can be smeared or stuck on small wall holds, or the points of the toe can be stuck into the crack in the hope that they will stay put.

*A finger jam with the thumb pressing the crack side to improve the security of the jam*

the natural jam. To hand jam, the back of the hand is pressed on to the wall of the crack by pressure on the opposite wall from finger tips and the thumb muscles, tensed by straightening the thumb and pressing it under the index finger. Fingers are kept straight, though the hand is bent at the knuckles. Sometimes climbers bend a thumb across their palm, but this is less effective than tensing the thumb. Hand jams can be used with the hand inverted or upright. Inverted feels most secure but the upright hand allows a greater reach for the next jam.

*Hand and fist cracks* are the commonest and most enjoyable of all jam cracks. Pure hand jamming is a joy to use in a rough parallel-sided crack just big enough to slide the hand in easily. If there are widenings in the crack, or narrowings, use these for natural jam placements. Even here, though, some jamming action with the hand is usually needed to aid

*A hand jam — most of the wedging work is done by the back of the hand and the thumb muscle*

John Sheard leads The Big Crack,
Froggatt Edge, Derbyshire

Jill Lawrence on Francine's Edge,
Buoux, France

*Mark Leach about to cut loose on the first free ascent of Kilnsey's Main Overhang, North Yorkshire*

*A foot jam*

*A fist jam*

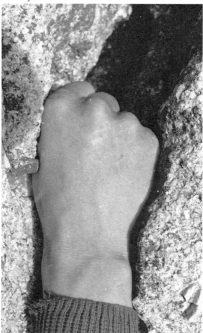

*An arm and shoulder jam (or 'arm bar') in an 'off-width' crack*

Frequently the best technique is to invert the upper hand while the lower hand remains upright.

Poor hand jams, e.g. when the crack is too narrow to allow the full hand to penetrate, are normally best tackled with the hand inverted. Wider cracks require the fist to be jammed crossways in the crack; put the hand in open then clench it at the appropriate place.

This jam feels much less secure that a hand jam. The crack in this type of jamming is usually wide enought for the foot to be jammed as well, greatly aiding the ascent. Feet are jammed by twisting the knee out sideways as the foot is raised and inserted into the crack. Twisting the knee back towards the crack jams the foot so that weight can be put on it.

*Off-width cracks* are the awful width between fist cracks and chimneys. Progress is slow and strenuous and is made by use of combinations of arm jams, pressure holds and foot or knee jams. If the crack is a corner crack it is normal to face the projecting wall; with a 'straight-in' crack one can face either way. The arm inside is jammed by pressing shoulder and elbow to one wall with the palm on the opposite wall. The other arm is usually low down, pressing up on the corner of the crack. The inside foot is wedged with the leg bent inside the crack, then the climber pushes up, wedges his outside foot near the

*Bridging a shallow overhanging groove turns a strenuous position into a resting position: Pete Gomersall on Profit of Doom (E4), Curbar Edge, Peak District*

*Bridging a groove: the left foot has just been raised, now the climber will lean on his right hand and raise his right foot*

edge of the crack, moves his inside leg higher and begins the process again. Variations like wedging the knee or wedging heel and toe across the crack can be used to advantage sometimes.

*Laybacking* is useful if the jams are poor and the crack is in a corner. With hands on the edge of the crack, leaning the body away from the crack, the feet can be walked up the opposite wall. A good rhythm with hand and feet moving at the same time can be achieved and it can be a very fast and effective, if strenuous, technique in certain situations. The steeper the layback crack becomes, the closer the feet have to be to the hands, and therefore the more strenuous it is. If the feet are too low they begin to slide down as the opposing pressures of hands and feet lose effectiveness.

## GROOVES AND CORNERS

The technique developed for climbing grooves and corners is called 'bridging'. It is similar to the straddling technique used in wide chimneys. The corner may or may not have a crack in the back; if it has then this can be used for hand jams while the feet find holds on either wall of the corner. Because it is possible to press outwards with the feet on to the walls of the corner, quite poor or small holds will suffice. As the upper part of the body is leaning into the corner and the feet are furthest out, the corner appears to be a lot less steep than it really is. It is frequently possible to take the hands off and rest them on an overhanging corner or groove if there are bridging holds for the feet.

Where there is no crack in the back of the corner, bridging holds have to be used for the hands as well. The hands are kept quite low down, sometimes just pressing on the wall without any definite hold. If the left foot is to be moved next, for intance, then the left hand should be dropped down lower than the right and this can be pushed on quite effectively so that the foot can be taken off and moved up. The left

hand is then moved up and the process repeated for the right-hand side. It is possible to use bridging techiques on almost flat walls or in very shallow grooves provided there are suitable footholds to press against. They can be valuable resting spots on steeper walls.

## ROOFS AND OVERHANGS

Roofs and overhangs are points where the rock suddenly sticks out like an inverted step. Roofs generally stick out at ninety degrees while overhangs can stick out at any angle. The size of roof on a free climbing route may be anything from twenty centimetres to twenty metres, though the bigger ones are only found on the harder climbs. Overhangs are generally easier than they appear; if a route crosses one you can bet there are excellent jams or good holds above it. No special technique is required, but the ability to pull over a roof on handholds alone then put a foot next to your hands certainly helps. Try and keep feet in contact with the rock all the time, at least then you are not carrying the weight of a pair of legs with your hands. Establishing oneself above the lip of a roof is usually the most difficult part; the trick is to get a foot on a hold just above the lip, then rock all your weight over on to that foot and stand up.

### Some general ideas on technique

Have a look at all the technique photos in the last two chapters, paying particular attention to hands and feet. You will notice that most photos show amazing similarities in the way that both are being used.

Hands are rarely to be seen above head height and are indeed frequently at shoulder height or below. Low hands mean that your body weight must be mainly where it should be – on your feet.

Look at the way feet are used; despite the wide variety of techniques being demonstrated, the inside of the foot between the tip of the big toe and the ball of the foot is the section most commonly in contact with the rock. Boot soles are almost always horizontal or sloping slightly downwards towards the heel and the heel points outwards away from the rock.

All these points add up to one main feature; that weight is on the feet and that the centre of gravity acts through the feet (i.e. in balance), rather than outside of the feet and therefore requiring arm strength to maintain equilibrium.

# 9 Leading 1

Leading is climbing and climbing is all about leading. That statement is true for the vast majority of climbers and it is the 'learning to lead' element of a climbing apprenticeship that marks the emergence of a climber able to operate independently.

So far this book has only talked about equipment and techniques with some mention of the desirability of high motivation in the trainee climber. These aspects contribute perhaps fifty per cent to the make-up of the complete climber. In leading we see the importance of the other fifty per cent: the mental qualities. Motivation, determination, coolness, anxiety, excitability are all facets of the climber's personality, and an awareness of these factors is an important factor in a successful leader's skill.

*Leading: a cool approach is required on protectionless slabs – Pink Void (E2), Baggy Point, Devon*

## LEADING QUALITIES

First of all, to lead you must really *want* to lead; wanting to do it, being self-motivated, is half the battle. When you have tried it, the extra satisfaction and thrill of leading rather than following will never be forgotten. Once at the sharp end of the rope, as the leader's end is called, the mental nature of the challenge becomes quite apparent – if not over-powering. You are immediately aware that if you fall off before you place your first runner you will hit the ground. Coolness is essential; any panic caused by too low an anxiety tolerance will immediately reduce your climbing standard or perhaps even root you to the spot, shaking. Even past the first runner you are still prey to the fear of falling; perhaps the runner is not the best, or the prospect of a short fall daunts you. 'Where does the route go?'; 'Am I going the right way?'; 'Am I strong enough to hang on all the way up the pitch?'; 'Will there be any more protection?' All these questions race through the leader's mind at some time or another and no matter what answer or action he decides upon, what he must *not* do is panic.

Determination to keep going and the ability to keep cool when things get exciting are qualities you must develop as a leader. The ability to lead grows with the confidence that comes from experience; confidence

unfounded on experience is soon rudely shattered and the leader brought down to earth – one way or another. You must also develop an awareness of the possibility of retreat should the climb prove impossible; it is a good idea when starting to lead always to check mentally that you can reverse a particular move or moves so that the last point of protection can be reached.

Sometimes on delicate slab climbing a high degree of concentration is required to make every move perfectly and without unnecessary movement that could cause feet to slip off. Again, you need a cool approach to be able to hold the necessary concentration. Many people do not possess these mental attributes naturally; but you can acquire them if you recognise the deficiency and are sufficiently motivated to try to overcome it. Careful confidence-building by climbing a series of routes that get gradually more difficult is one way to help develop leading qualities.

First leads should always be on climbs considerably easier than those which the leader is capable of seconding. The good, experienced leader, however, should expect to be able to lead climbs of the same grade as those he can second.

## GUIDEBOOKS AND GUIDES

Leading consists not only of going first up the climb but also of finding the crag, choosing and locating a suitable climb and following the line of a climb. Most cliffs or climbing areas are covered by a rock climbing guidebook. These books are available from most climbing equipment shops, especially those in or near the area to be visited. They are written by active climbers from the area and revised every few years as new climbs are ascended. They contain descriptions of the area and how to get to the various crags, some historical notes on first ascents and notable achievements, and most importantly, a description of every route in the area covered by the guide. Each route is graded for difficulty and its length given, as is the position of the start and some indication of the line the climb follows. Depending on the area the route description may be quite vague, e.g. 'Climb upwards following cracks for two or three pitches', or very detailed, e.g. 'Step up and left to a good hold, then back right to a finger crack.' The former leaves much of the route-finding work to the climber, while the latter is the kind of description found in guides to shorter outcrop crags. Guides have lots of set phrases that the novice leader will rapidly become familiar with, although they may be a little bewildering for a start; the main thing is to look for the natural line.

*A word of warning:* guidebooks are frequently based on information supplied by other climbers and this is not always checked by the guidebook editors; grades and comments on the difficulty of routes should be treated with caution when using a guide, especially on newer routes.

An increasingly popular form of guidebook is the 'topo guide'; this is simply a line drawing of the route with symbols to denote various features such as corners and overhangs. A drawing of the cliff itself is also usually included so that the start of the route may be identified.

*Interpretation*

Pitch 8: *climb easily rightwards along the summit ridge.*

Pitch 7: *easy climbing leads leftwards up a ridge to gain the summit ridge.*

Pitch 6: *climb the corner for 50m to its end.*

Pitch 5: *climb the crack, then a slab to a stance below a corner.*

Pitch 4: *traverse right and down from the stance to enter a chimney. Climb this for 50m, exiting right at the top to a stance below a crack.*

Pitch 3: *Move onto the right wall of the corner and ascend for 20m to a stance below a roof.*

Pitch 2: *climb the long difficult corner straight above for 50m.*

Pitch 1: *cliimb the left side of the pillar for 50m, entering a corner after 20m.*

*Climb easily diagonally leftwards to the start (S) at a grassy patch on the left side of a large pillar.*

## ROUTE FINDING

An ability to interpret the guidebook, only gained by experience, is the most important characteristic of the successful route finder. Once you have located the start of the route from the guidebook, read the preamble to the route description; this frequently describes the nature of the route's line, e.g. 'This climb follows the steep leftward-facing corner before escaping on to the buttress on the right.' With this introduction, look for the general line of the route; maybe it will be very obvious. Once on the route, follow the guidebook description, but at the same time try to take the natural or easiest line to reach an objective. Routes that avoid the natural easy line deliberately are called 'eliminates'. Look out for signs of earlier traffic; holds are frequently polished, scratched or blackened from long use, and the line itself may be cleaner than the rock round about. On harder routes, smudges of chalk frequently mark the handholds, giving excellent clues to the route and even how to climb it. If you find yourself on a section of climbing that is much harder than the grade you expected, then the first thing is to check that you are in the right place — if not, retreat. Perhaps there are much harder but more obvious lines using the same start as your route: check with the guide.

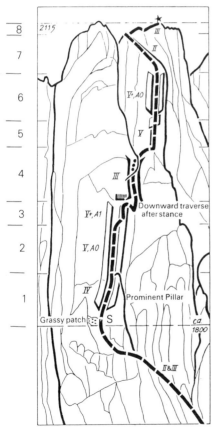

A 'topo' route description — the Predigstuhl West Face, Austria

Ways of grading climbs for difficulty are numerous and confusing, mainly because of the very egocentric nature of leading climbers and first ascensionists who like their own ways of grading climbs. Individual climbers consistently either undergrade or overgrade climbs, while others use a grading system in an unconventional way. All very confusing: the British grading system, though, is now fairly well established and has two sections (see pages 159-160). An adjectival grade gives an overall indication of the difficulty and seriousness of the route. The numerical grade is purely a technical grade to indicate the difficulty of a particular section of the climb (usually each pitch).

Normally VS routes have no pitch harder than 4c and HVS routes have no pitch harder than 5b. A climb graded HVS but with virtually no protection for the leader could have 4a technical grades, while a well-protected, short-lived VS could have a 5a pitch on it. *Remember:* grades are only an indication of difficulty and something to talk and argue about afterwards.

*The first ascent of Oriole, Crafnant Valley, North Wales: Pete Gomersall climbing a thin 5 c pitch*

## PROTECTION

The art of placing protection is the most important technical skill a leader has to learn. Equipment and techniques have progressed so rapidly in this field over the last few years that what was a fairly simple matter is now a quite complex and constantly developing skill. Even quite recent textbooks are rapidly outdated in this field. If a leader falls off, protection is what stops him hitting the ground or makes his fall as short as possible. Thirty years ago it was almost unthinkable that a leader should fall: such were the limitations of the protection techniques then in use that he ran a serious risk of fatal injury if he did. Nowadays it is quite common for a leader to fall, especially on the harder routes, and yet climbing is much safer than it was twenty years ago. The two most important innovations have been the development of 'nuts', the art of placing them (known as 'chockcraft') and the widespread use of expansion bolts for protection. Better ropes, lighter equipment, belay plates, harnesses and expanding protection devices have all helped to further development. A leader could, on certain climbs, easily fix running belays by hammering pitons or expansion bolts into the climb at various points, but that would make the climb substantially easier and would damage the rock. This kind of ascent is not

*Perfect confidence-boosting protection in exactly the right place for the crux move on Profit of Doom (E4), Curbar Edge, Peak District*

acceptable in rock climbing and the advice generally given in guidebooks is that if a leader is tempted to place a piton or bolt he should get off and try an easier climb.

There are various crucial links between a leader, his second and his anchor. These lines are called the belay chain. All the links have to stand various amounts of shock loading should the leader fall, but the points that have to take most strain are the leader's protection points, his runners. Placements for main anchors such as slings on spikes and blocks, threads, nuts, pitons or bolts will of course also make ideal running belays and all the previous information on anchors holds good for runners. Sometimes pitons or bolts will be found in place for runners: such instances are usually mentioned in the guidebook.

To be effective, therefore, good protection must be in the right place to stop a leader falling a long way, good enough to give a leader confidence, easily fixed and not damaging to the rock. It must also stop the falling leader from hitting the ground or an intermediate ledge. Very important also, and not as humorous as it sounds, protection must not fall out as soon as the leader has passed it! So you must learn the art of connecting the nut or runner to the main rope so that the protection is not lifted out.

## LEARNING TO LEAD

Some people are quite happy just to go and lead almost as soon as they start climbing, learning protection techniques as they go along. For most of us, however, a rather safer, steadier way is advisable. A gradual introduction to leading might be as follows:

1 Gain experience as a second, removing protection and fixing belays to the anchors at stances under the eye of your leader.

2 Climb a suitable easy, well-protected route (usually a one-pitch route) as a second, leaving the protection in place.

3 Lead the route, clipping into the protection.

4 Practise putting in protection at ground level.

5 Second another easy route.

6 Lead it, inserting your own protection, perhaps having it checked as you go by a more competent climber.

7 Lead an easy climb that you have not climbed before; at this point you will begin to feel the true elation of leading climbs.

A further step could be added between steps 5 and 6: climbing down the route top-roped from above, inserting protection as you go – but this stage is not usually necessary. Other options involve your mentor, whether he be guide, instructor or friend, watching you from the top of the climb with a spare rope that can be lowered to you as a top rope should the need arise. When a leader can fix protection quickly and efficiently and have confidence in it he should start to raise his leading standard to approach his seconding ability, and from then on leading and seconding standards should advance apace.

# 10    *Leading 2*

## PROTECTION TECHNIQUES

The aims of a leader securing protection are threefold: most importantly, the aim is to fix runners in a climb so that should we fall we would not hit the ground, a ledge nor even a bulging section of the cliff below. Secondly, protection is used to enhance the confidence of the leader; protection placed at the crux of a pitch is very comforting psychologically, especially if it can be placed high above the climber's head at the crux, thus turning the move into a virtual top rope situation. Thirdly, protection offers the leader the possibility of retreat by being lowered to the ledge or ground from the highest piece of protection. This is both a real help if required and a psychological help during the climb itself.

Unfortunately, protecting the leader is in reality far from ideal; some climbs are virtually unprotectable, forcing the leader to make a serious decison before commencing the climb about whether or not this is really the climb for him. On other climbs protection is not available in the ideal textbook places and the leader must take what opportunities are available. Nor is protection always of the strength one would normally wish for; often you have to ask yourself whether it is better to use up a nut on poor protection now or carry on hoping for better further up the pitch.

Protection techniques are a skill in themselves, combining knowledge of strengths and optimum placings of runners: placing protection; speed of placement and organisation of equipment. Once the basic idea of what the leader is trying to do has been mastered, lots of practice is needed to improve efficiency and competence in the art. It is another key skill in the leader's survival kit.

## EQUIPMENT AND CARRYING IT

A climber's collection of gear for protection is called his 'rack'. Nowadays a rack consists of varying numbers of nuts, karabiners and tape slings. To be sure of always having a nut to fit every crack on the route a climber would have to carry a ridiculously large quantity of equipment. Every nut needs a karabiner, so the poor climber would probably be unable to leave the ground, so heavy would his rack be. A compromise is reached, between five and fifteen nuts being the sort of quantity it is usual to carry these

*A typical rack of nuts; from left to right, hexentrics, wedges on rope and wired wedges – fourteen in all*

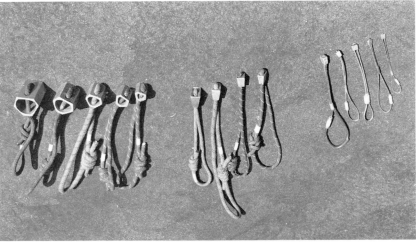

days. The average climb uses a range of sizes, so the rack has a range of nuts from 5 mm to 80 mm in width; one of each making a rack of ten or eleven nuts. In addition, a few expanding cam devices may push the size range up to 150 mm or so, as well as adding flexibility to the range. Unusual climbs may have nuts in one size range only; perhaps only small nuts would be carried, but two or three of each size would make up the rack. Of course other variables come into it; length of pitch or difficulty are taken into account when deciding what to carry. A short slab climb requires very little to be carried, whereas a long crack pitch may need a full rack of, say, fifteen nuts. Each nut should have its own snaplink karabiner which is fastened either to carrying loops on a waist harness or to a tape bandolier carried across the shoulder.

The number of tape slings to be carried depends very much on the nature of the climbing, but for rock that sports inviting-looking spikes or trees a selection of two long (double) slings and three shorter slings, each with a krab, would be appropriate. In addition a few quick draws should be carried. The slings are worn across the shoulder (on the opposite shoulder and on top of the rack bandolier), while quick draws are fastened to the harness or bandolier.

Nuts should be arranged on the rack in order of size and nuts threaded onto rope should have

rope of a different colour for each size to help speedy identification. Practise closing your eyes and selecting the exact size you want for a particular crack (while still on the ground of course!).

A normal range of nuts would contain perhaps four wedge-shaped nuts on wire; these would be the smallest four in the rack and would be fairly close in size. Next

A harness racking system with the smallest nuts to the front

would be three or four wedge-shaped nuts threaded on rope. The smallest of these should have holes large enough to accept 5 mm rope; any smaller and the nut is better on wire. The largest nuts should be a range of about four hexagonal nuts, usually hollow for lightness and with quite a large size differential between them. Nuts should be as versatile as

A bandolier racking system: easy to swap racks, but does tend to get in the way and obscure vision of footwork

possible; wedges, for instance, should have a taper on both sets of sides so that they will fit two sizes of crack. The best kind of hexagon nut is the Polycentric, which will fit two crack sizes.

Expanding cam devices (typically Friends, Flexible Friends and Quadcams) come in four or five sizes with half sizes between. A normal useful starter range would be four or five of the full sizes; the styles with solid stems are inherently stronger and easier to use, but their propensity to lose strength dramatically if a horizontal stem is loaded downwards over an edge should always be remembered.

If climbing in 'bolt areas' such as France and Germany much of the information here is irrelevant, for there a rack consists of a couple of slings and up to twenty quick draws (each with two krabs). However, routes which are solely bolt-protected tend to be in the upper grades: only the fit and agile will advance directly to bolt routes and so avoid an apprenticeship of chockcraft and conventional protection techniques. Even for these people there are excellent reasons for learning all about nuts; many of the world's finest climbs are not bolt-protected and never will be, and many of the unforeseen incidents that happen in rock climbing will take you away from the safety of the shiny secure lifeline of a bolt ladder.

## SPACING OF NUTS

It is important to realise how far one will fall before being arrested by the rope running through protection. If a climber is five metres above the karabiner on a nut, then he will fall twice that five metres, plus a few metres for

*An effective top roping situation created by protection high above the leader's head*

stretch in the rope, plus a few metres for any slack in the belay system to be absorbed. So he may fall $5 + 5 + 2 + 2 = 14$ metres. He will end up nine metres below the krab on the nut, not much use if the ground was only eight metres below the nut. So the theory of protection placement is this: protection is only effective if it stops you hitting the ground (or a large ledge); always try to place another before getting so high above the last one that you may hit the ground.

In practice we tend to place nuts wherever we can get them, but sometimes we have a choice. A nut five metres up is only good until a climber is not quite three metres above it. If another is then placed at eight metres, then this is good until the climber is four and a half metres above the top nut. The top nut then would be at twelve and a half metres. The further up you get, the bigger the gap that is possible between pieces of protection. Other factors play a part, though; the thought of a long fall is very frightening, so gaps between nuts should never get very large. A nut placed on the crux of the pitch is psychologically very helpful, no matter how close it is to the last one. If the nut is a bad one, then the first good placement afterwards should be utilised. Do not leave bad nuts unplaced because they are poor – even if they only absorb some of the energy in a fall before coming out they will have helped. A good stopper nut (i.e. one that is strong and mechanically sound, sure to stop you) should be placed as soon as possible after leaving a stance that is above the ground, or on the ground but above a steep slope. This will prevent the belayer being loaded directly with the force of a falling leader; instead he will experience an upward pull. In fact, it would frequently be possible to lace a climb from top to bottom with a huge amount of nuts, all placed above the climber so that he never got into an 'above the nut' position. This would entail a lot of weight on the rack, − but more important, it is perhaps unethical to beat a climb by so overprotecting it that the leader is in effect top roped.

The leader who can place his nuts quickly by fast selection, placing and clipping in, can be fairly confident that he can place nuts at any stage of the climb, no matter how strenuous the situation. The less experienced and practised leader will have to place his nuts at rest places only, or in sections where the climb is not too strenuous.

### Extending protection

We extend protection for two reasons: to help stop it dropping out after we have climbed above it, and to reduce rope drag caused by protection 'out of line' putting bends in the rope − bends in the line of the rope tend to pull slings off and nuts out anyway. Pegs and bolts only need to be lengthened to reduce rope drag − hopefully they will not be lifted out. We should avoid extending protection to cut down the length of potential fall and therefore reduce runner loading. The answer therefore has to be a thoughtful compromise.

It is obviously pointless to extend runners that are close to the ground or a ledge if to lengthen them means that you would hit the ground. These low runners are redundant anyway once you are a metre or so above them − so it doesn't matter if they drop out.

As a general rule, always lengthen wire nuts unless lengthening would make them obsolete for protection. Lengthen other forms of protection to stop 'lifting out' of protection or reduce rope drag, but only lengthen by the minimum amount required to do the job: that way the size of potential fall is kept to a minimum.

### RUNNER STRENGTH

There is no point in using a strong and heavy krab on a nut that has thin (therefore relatively weak) rope. A runner is only as strong as its weakest link, which could be the rock, the chock itself, the wire or cord threading the chock, the karabiner or even an extension sling between the nut and main climbing rope. Good protection technique aims for links of equal strength so that extra weight is not carried and wasted, and the best use is made of available protection placements. A good solid spike or nut placement therefore needs a strong sling or nut to avoid weak links. Conversely, a poor spike or crumbling nut placement only warrants a lightweight sling or lightweight krab on the nut.

Smaller nuts are threaded with thinner wire; on the very smallest this wire can have a quite low breaking strain. These smallest nuts should therefore be regarded as useful only to protect a move or two, and not as a mainstay component of a pitch's sequence of protection − in other words it is an 'extra' for a difficult move. In normal circumstances you would always lengthen a wired nut to provide a flexible link and prevent dislodgement, but with a thin wire only intended for a move or two it is frequently best to omit the extension and clip straight into the wire. This reduces the length of potential fall and therefore the shock loading experienced at the nut, but it does increase the likelihood of the nut dropping out after you have passed it.

Generally speaking, good spikes with full strength tape, good nut placements or good pitons are as strong as other parts of the belay chain and runners such as these may be used in confidence. Weaknesses to watch out for are flakes which sound hollow or are cracked at the base; and rusted *in situ* pegs, *in situ* slings or nuts, where exposure to weather eventually destroys the strength of the nylon. *In situ* tapes or nuts are litter anyway, and should be removed if possible.

## PLACING PROTECTION

The organisation of a leader's rack of nuts, quick draws and slings is the first step towards effective protection placement. The leader climbing at his limit will at some time find himself in a position in which it is difficult to let go with one hand to place protection. The position may be very strenuous, not a place to stop for long, but may also be the only place for a decent piece of protection. It is in these situations that the climber must be able to position his body and balance so that a hand may be taken off the rock, then must be able to unclip from his waist and place a piece of protection, preferably in one fluid movement without even looking at the rack. The achieve this the rack must be well ordered in size, probably with small nuts and quick draws at the front, graduating to large nuts and Friends at the back; a leader who knows his rack well will be able to unclip a particular piece without looking. The other part of the technique concerns the ability to look at the rock feature or crack and estimate accurately the correct tape or suitably sized nut for the situation.

*Extending protection to reduce rope drag*

## Tapes

Tapes are carried across the shoulder or around the neck if shorter; double tapes should be a different colour from single tapes and each should be clipped with a snaplink krab. If screwgate krabs are used they should not be screwed up (locked) until they are actually in use on the main rope. For a spike or block of rock, pick a tape that is plenty long enough so that the krab hangs down well below the rock anchor. This helps to prevent the tape from lifting off inadvertently and keeps the mechanical loading on the sling within reasonable limits. The sling should be 'seated' on the spike so that it will not slide off if loaded and will not be cut on sharp edges of rock.

When a tape is to be threaded around a jammed block or through an eyehole, it should be gripped at the opposite end from the krab and knot and threaded so that this section need not be pulled through the thread. The two ends are then clipped together with a krab. When removing threads, care should be taken not to pull the tape hard, but to ease it out gently, as tape has a habit of jamming itself into places where you can't get at it.

Once placed, a tape draped over a spike should be passed carefully; violent or jerky movements of the knees or rope are highly likely to lift the tape off its spike. Once a few metres above, however, this problem is unlikely to occur. (The same also applies to moving up past some loose nut placements).

## Chockcraft

In general, all nuts are best placed above narrowings in a crack to give a good natural jamming action. This kind of placement is essential with wedge-shaped nuts but hexagonal nuts work reasonably well in nearly parallel cracks due to a 'camming' action. Some general points about nut placement are:

☐ Check the nut is resting against the walls of the crack and not on small dimple-like rugosities that may break off.

☐ Beware of placements in cracks or holes where the rock is shattered; the nut may pull away under load.

☐ Use the largest nut that will fit the situation.

☐ Work out the direction of a possible pull and see if the nut is good for a pull that way.

☐ Beware of placing nuts behind flakes or in cracks that may 'expand' under load.

☐ Check knots on slings before climbing, they can work loose easily.

☐ Don't use up all the nuts of one size range if you can see you may need one higher up the pitch.

☐ Although all nuts can be placed in a crack two ways, either lengthways or widthways, the narrowest way is safest as the nut is generally more stable in that position.

*Wedges* are best inserted in vertical or diagonal cracks above a constriction or above a bend in the crack that stops the nut slipping down. Cracks narrower at the entrance are better but make removing the wedge more difficult. A bit of stiff wire or a special nut-removing tool is sometimes useful for removing nuts. Check the security of a wedged nut by giving it a little jerk to wedge it in place.

*A wedge in a good natural jamming position*

The wedge should be completely inside the crack, not rocking loosely half in and half out. It should also have as many parts of its body in contact with the rock as possible: this helps stabilise the nut and is also stronger. Many modern wedges have concave faces to improve the possibility of getting secure points of contact in uneven cracks – they seem to work well.

*Hexagonal nuts* (Hexentrics, Polycentrics) are a little more awkward to place. Because of their shape they need to be tilted to one side slightly to present the narrowest cross-section to the crack. Once wedged in place a load on the rope tends to twist the nut, making it bite even harder into the crack walls; this action is called 'camming'. In cracks with fairly

*A 'hex' in use in a vertical crack*

A 'hex' used crossways

parallel sides the nut must be a tight fit to hold it in place when there is no load on it. Camming nuts work well in horizontal cracks; slide them in sideways until they jam. They should be placed in such a way that the sling exits from the nut closer to the roof of the crack than the floor. When load is applied, the downward pull activites the camming action.

*Wired nuts* (wedges) are the easiest of all nuts to place because they can be worked into the correct position easily by manipulating the wire − a kind of remote-control placement.

They can be placed in cracks above that are out of reach by using the wire to gain extra reach, or placed deep in narrow cracks that the fingers cannot reach. Unfortunately, the stiff wire on these nuts makes them dislodge much more easily and extra care is needed when connecting the nut to the main rope to avoid dislodgement by jerks on the rope. Even knocking the wire with a foot as one passes can inadvertently remove a wired nut. Hexagonal nuts on wire are less useful as the stiffness of the wire prevents the camming action from working effectively.

*Always lengthen a wired nut*

*A 'hex' in a horizontal crack: note how a downward pull increases the camming action*

*Christine Walker leading the Left Unconquerable at Stanage Edge, Derbyshire*

*Royal Robbins climbing in Teluride, Colorado*

*Jill Lawrence soloing the striking ridge of Dentelles de Montmirail*

*Nuts in opposition*    If a climb traverses into a crack, then goes straight up, any nut placed at the bottom of the crack would be pulled upwards by the rope and so dislodged. To prevent this the nut is tensioned downwards by an upward-facing nut placed lower in the crack. The sling length which will obtain the correct tension is adjusted by tying overhand knots in the lower sling. In horizontal cracks a normal downward pull results in the nut being pulled directly outwards. Horizontal cracks are frequently without suitable placements for this type of pull, but if two nuts are positioned facing each other the sling of one nut can be threaded through a krab on the other sling. The net effect of a load on the threaded sling is to pull both nuts along the line of the crack, i.e. the kind of pull normally experienced in vertical cracks.

*Stacking*    Two wedge nuts can be quite effectively stacked together to form a wider wedge. Although difficult to arrange, the resulting placement works well in almost parallel cracks. The smaller wedge points uphill with the load on the downward-pointing larger one. In practice, however, stacking is hardly ever used; it is fiddly to arrange and there is nearly always an alternative, i.e. an expanding cam device. It should be regarded as a technique to be used in emergencies or when no other option exists.

*Nut removal*    Speedy and effective removal of nuts is necessary to conserve strength and avoid littering the crags with jammed nuts. Most wedges fly out with a gentle upward jerk. If they fail to move after the first jerk they should be loosened with the fingers and gently wriggled out. Never try and force a nut out – it will usually jam harder. Hexagonal camming nuts are best removed by gently loosening and wriggling outwards with the fingers; pulling only operates the camming action. For difficult nuts a piece of stiff wire with a doubled end about 200 mm long is useful. If bent into a semicircle, the wire can also be used for pulling slings through awkward threads or eyeholes.

Purpose-made nut-removal tools are available; some also help in removing expanding cam devices such as Friends, but they are 'dedicated' items of gear in that they can only be used for this task – so a piece of stiff wire may be more useful.

*Nuts in opposition: the pull on each nut is towards the krab in the middle, whereas an outward pull on either side might dislodge it*

*Stacking nuts: the downward-pointing one only is connected to the climbing rope*

*Expanding cam devices*   These rather complex and mechanical-looking devices have several key uses as a substitute for ordinary nuts where an ordinary nut won't hold, or where you have no nut of the correct size. The two situations in which they are most useful are in outward and downward 'flaring' cracks (cracks that get wider downwards or outwards) where no normal nut will ever stick.

They are also useful in perfectly parallel cracks where other nuts would be difficult to lodge; and regular cracks that may take a nut, but where the pull is directly outwards, also provide expanding cam placements.

As a general rule the devices with rigid stems are stronger and hold better, so should be used in most situations. The exception is any situation where the pull on the stem is not in line with the length of the stem – most commonly found in horizontal placements where the stem sticks out from the crack. A flexible stem here would bend into line with the load.

There are several points to bear in mind when placing these devices:

☐ Always align the stem and cam with the direction of loading.

☐ Make sure the cams are symmetrical with each other when viewed from the side – a pair of cams that are offset have little holding power.

☐ Avoid placements where the cam is wide open with only the tips in contact with the rock.

☐ Have a flexible link between stem and climbing rope – a shaking rope can cause a

*A 'Friend' in a flared crack useless for a conventional nut*

*A horizontal placement with a 'Friend' placed deep into the crack to avoid a bending action on the stem*

device to 'walk' into the crack and be irretrievable or move to a section of crack that is too wide.

- ☐ Don't force an overlarge cam into a crack − it will be difficult to remove.

- ☐ Cams can be difficult to remove from bottoming or blind cracks as removal is effected by pulling the trigger and pushing the device inwards to release it at the same time; cams in cracks that have bottomed can't be pushed inwards.

- ☐ Four camming surfaces are generally more reliable than two or three.

## ROPE SYSTEMS

There are two commonly used rope systems today: one involves a single 11 mm rope and the other two 9 mm ropes. Although the techniques used are rather different for the two systems, the aim is the same. Effective rope technique is one which safely connects the leader to his second and his protection in the form of runners. It also minimises drag, experienced by the leader due to

*Without lengthening the runners there is considerable drag with this single-rope system*

bends in the rope as it passes projections and runners. Finally, it is a technique which affords good protection in a fall to either leader or second.

## Single-rope system

This is the system most commonly used by beginners. Routes frequently follow a zigzag line and pass corners, projections or overhangs. If the rope is passed through runners it forces the rope to bend and rub against projections as the leader climbs. The dragging effect on the leader can be so great that he is unable to move, to say nothing of the likelihood of runners dislodging because the rope pulls them sideways. To avoid both these problems it is necessary to lengthen some of the runners by adding an extra sling and karabiner to allow the main rope to run as straight as possible. Of course some bends will always exist, and it should be borne in mind that some runners become useless if lengthened too much. Remember that lengthening a runner by a metre increases the leader's potential fall by just over two metres. Wired nuts in particular need a flexible link between them and the main rope;

*The drag is lessened by lengthening certain runners and thereby straightening the run of the rope*

at the very least two linked karabiners should be used. Nuts or fixed pitons and bolts in the corner underneath a roof should always be lengthened so that the rope is not bent as it passes over the lip of the overhang.

If a pitch involves traversing and then some vertical ascent the leader should try to avoid fixing protection at the end of the traverse or on the first bit of vertical ascent, as when the second follows, the rope will go uphill from him as he traverses and not horizontally to the end of the traverse; this could result in a nasty pendulum fall if he slipped.

## Double-rope systems

These have several advantages over the single rope, but they are rather more difficult for the belayer to manipulate – and of course two 9 mm ropes are a lot more expensive than one 11 mm rope. The basic idea with a double-rope system is that the climber should clip into alternate runners with each rope, so that each rope is subjected to less bends. The two ropes should be different colours to avoid confusion when clipping in and communicating with the belayer. On intricate zig-zagging pitches the ropes should look like a pair of railway lines. To achieve this

*A double-rope system in use in the Rheinpfalz, West Germany*

*Using double ropes, the traverse in the middle of Walewska is protected for both leader and second*

effect it is sometimes necessary to clip one rope into two consecutive runners if they are in line with each other; then perhaps the other rope would be clipped into the next runner or two if they are offset. Ideally, however, you should clip into alternate runners with each rope because since a 9 mm rope is thinner than an 11 mm rope it will stretch more with the force of a falling leader. This has two possible effects: on a poor runner the extra energy absorbed by the rope is less likely to pull the runner out and gives less of a jerk to the faller; but on the other hand, a stretched 9 mm rope is much more likely to cut itself in two if it lies across a sharp edge when the faller's weight is on it.

A good second using the double-rope system only pays out each rope as it is needed and also takes in slack in each rope as it appears. Good ropework with a double rope generally means that the falling leader will not fall as far or swing as much as the leader on a single rope. Less extra gear is required for lengthening, and with less lengthening falls are potentially shorter. If a fall does occur then the double rope is held and belayed as though it were a single rope; it is generally easier to hold than a single rope. In situations where retreat is necessary, the double rope has twice the length and is therefore much more useful.

The advantages of a double-rope system become more apparent as the climbing gets more complex and difficult and as the leader pushes his limits more closely. Pitches become longer and more devious, just clipping into protection may be an effort and the protection itself may be of marginal value. In these situations a good leader and second can use double ropes to great effect: a good runner one metre down can be clipped to one rope, while the other can be paid out to clip a poor runner two metres about the climber's waist. If a fall now occurs the runner may hold and the leader stops in place; if the runner fails then the leader falls two metres to be held by the lower nut on the other rope. Using a single rope system the same scenario would produce a fall of ten metres or so, frightening and considerably increasing the chances of injury.

It is possible to fall off when trying to clip a bolt or peg above your head. A single-rope system introduces a potentially large amount of slack into the system, so dramatically increasing the fall length. A double-rope system always has the leader falling onto the last runner, with no extra slack in the system, thereby minimising the length of fall.

*Traverses* are made safer for both leader and second with a double rope. It is usually possible to arrange the ropes so that the second has a rope going up above him as he does the traverse, while the other rope has been used by the leader to protect the end section of the traverse. Falls on traverses are normally pendulum-type falls with the leader swinging in an arc below the runner. This kind of fall puts much less strain on a runner than a vertical fall, so poor runners are frequently good enough for traversing falls, even though they might have been useless for straight falls.

### Choosing a rope system

Single ropes are stronger than a double rope when the full force of a fall comes onto only one of the double ropes; they are also cheaper and are much simpler to operate. The double-rope system is inherently safer, more flexible and helps you to reach optimum performance by lessening drag and improving confidence through better use of runners. Some climbs, notably the straight granite cracks of the Western U.S.A. or the bolt ladder protection of parts of Europe, are quite suited to single ropes because of their straight nature. For all-round, all-out performance and flexibility, the double-rope system has to be best.

## Fall factors

Different kinds of fall apply different forces to the leader. Some knowledge of how these forces arise and how to manipulate them will enable the leader to minimise the force experienced by him or her during a fall. The severity of a fall is also a key factor in deciding whether or not to retire a rope. The concept of fall severity – called the fall factor – is shown by the relationship:

$$\text{Fall factor} = \frac{\text{length of fall}}{\text{length of rope available to absorb fall}}$$

– in other words, a fall of a particular length will produce a particular amount of energy; the more rope there is available to absorb this energy, the lower will be the fall factor.

If a climber leads 10 m above a belay ledge and falls without intermediate protection, his fall length will be 20 m and the 'available rope' is 10 m. The fall factor is therefore:

$$\frac{20}{10} = 2$$

Two is the worst possible fall factor encountered in normal climbing situations and should be avoided at all costs. A runner at 5 m above the ledge would reduce the fall factor:

$$\frac{10}{10} = 1$$

while a runner at 8 m would reduce the fall factor still further:

$$\frac{4}{10} = 0.4$$

Thus a short 4 m fall with no runners can produce a fall factor of 2, whereas a 20 m fall at the end of a long pitch can produce a fall factor of say:

$$\frac{20}{40} = 0.5$$

which is a quite acceptable figure as far as forces on the rope and leader are concerned – though the equation ignores the considerable discomfort that may be felt by hitting a ledge or rock face on the way down.

As a general rule, always keep the fall factor below 1.

# 11 *Training for climbing*

Training for climbing is a relatively new idea. Traditionally, the only practice that climbers had was the climbing itself. In some areas bouldering was done in the evenings as an end in itself, though it also provided useful training for roped climbing.

The purposes and aims of training are centred around improving performance of the activity in question in the most efficient manner. To many climbers this kind of clinical approach to improving climbing performance is anathema to their view of the sport of climbing, and it is not being suggested here that all climbers *should* train or that training is suitable for all climbers; you can have a highly enjoyable and successful lifetime in climbing with nothing more than the initial skills of climbing. There are, however, two things to be said in favour of training:

☐ If you want to improve your climbing standard then training is by far the most effective way to do it. Improving one's standard brings much personal satisfaction and pleasure; it also opens up much more scope and choice in terms of climbs and the climbing areas that become accessible.

☐ The fitness acquired through training is rather more general than that acquired through normal climbing activities. The sense of well-being and physical competency it gives when climbing adds greatly to the enjoyment of climbing. There is a great feeling of freedom of movement when one is less constrained by physical shortcomings.

If, then, you decide that some training is worth while you might as well discover the most effective way of training so that you gain the maximum output. As in all sports there are people who are 'trainers' rather than 'climbers', who spend all their time training for climbing, but rarely climb. This chapter is not for them; it is for those who simply wish to climb as well as possible.

## GENERAL PRINCIPLES

There are several key concepts in training that must be grasped before concentrating specifically on climbing training. They are:

☐ *Performance analysis* – analysing climbing to discuss what components make up performance and what the features of those components are, e.g. muscle groups involved, duration of effort.

☐ *Specificity* – training should be specific to the activity in terms of skills, muscle groups, range of movement, energy systems.

☐ *Energy systems* – there are three: two are anaerobic (they work without oxygen from the lungs) and one aerobic (which works with oxygen). For very short-term effort of up to twenty seconds the ATP-PC (adenosine triphosphate-phosphocreatine) system is used; it is based on a chemical reaction between stored chemicals at the muscle. For work of up to two minutes in duration the Lactic Acid system (LA-02) comes into play. This again uses stored chemicals, but the duration of the system is limited by the capacity of the muscle to tolerate the by-product of the reaction, lactic acid.

Aerobic work involves the oxygen energy system which uses inhaled oxygen, carried by the blood to the muscle, and the nutrient conversion and transport system which converts food calories into energy carriers which are transported again via the blood to the muscles. Given regular nutrient and oxygen supply the aerobic energy system is long-term, but it is more limited than the anaerobic system in the intensity level of the work that can be done.

☐ *Muscle fibres* – are of two basic types, white fibres which work with anaerobic energy systems and red fibres which work with the oxygen energy system. We each have a different balance of the fibre types which determines our muscles' potential for one type of work or another, but training can alter the apparent balance.

☐ *Overload* – is an intensity of exercise above the normal and is essential for training to take place. Overload does not mean maximal work output though, but some percentage of that figure, usually in the seventy to eighty per cent zone.

☐ *Intensity, duration and frequency* – are training parameters. Intensity is the level of work load, duration is the length of time that work load is sustained and frequency the number of training sessions per week.

☐ *Repetitions* – are the number of times a particular exercise is repeated. There may or may not be a rest between each repetition. A specific number of repetitions is a *set*. The repetition maximum (R.M.) is the maximum load that can be tolerated for a particular set of repetitions. Training regimes normally work at some submaximal percentage of R.M.

☐ *Evaluating progression* – the advantage of carefully constructed training regimes is that progress can easily be monitored, allowing the R.M. figure to be updated every so often and so updating the training intensity without increasing overload. A diary should be kept recording progress.

☐ *Strength* – is the maximum force that a muscle can exert at any one time. It is not the same as 'work', which includes duration of force in the equation. If you can't pull up on a small hold at the start of a climb, or do a one-leg high step-up without hand assistance, then it is your strength that needs working on. Note that after some strenuous effort the ability to pull up is not related to pure strength but to other factors related to fatigue.

☐ *Flexibility* – an extremely important and trainable aspect of climbing performance that has until recently gone largely unnoticed. Mainly it increases the number of holds available for use and increases the efficiency of movement by enabling effective body position adjustment and increasing the effectiveness and range of muscle use on a particular joint.

☐ *Mental training* – in climbing this is mainly about learning to control anxiety. Motivational training in climbing is probably unethical – in most of its forms it is not in the spirit of climbing.

It becomes obvious that climbing performance, and therefore training, has several different aspects which could be worked upon; to improve performance most effectively, however, start by working on the weakest component of performance. Poor components of performance have much greater improvement potential than aspects in which you are already fit. There is also a detrimental psychological spin-off in the knowledge that you have a 'weak link'.

## COMPONENTS OF CLIMBING PERFORMANCE

There are two aspects to understanding climbing performance; first we must identify the nature of the demands made by the rock and the routes, and second we must look at the nature of our own performance in climbing and its compatibility with the former.

The first thing to realise is that climbing is a very diverse activity in terms of its physiological demands on the individual; hence bouldering demands a totally different kind of training from that required for the ascent of Himalayan peaks, and the two forms of training have little or no compatibility or overlap. Here we are concerned with analysing as narrow a band of activity as possible: the range from bouldering to crag climbing. Even here it must be pointed out that bouldering may be substantially different in its training demands from multi-pitch crag climbing. Furthermore, different types of routes, e.g. easy or hard, overhanging jugs or vertical tiny holds, will demand different training regimes because of their differing performance properties.

*Bouldering* Arm and finger strength and skill are the main requirements. The energy system is exclusively anaerobic (ATP-PC), but it is not an important factor in bouldering, which is a 'one move' performance.

*Short one-pitch climbs* Some skill and some strength are needed, especially for those

*The ATP-PC energy system is used for short bursts of work on this short climb: Maupassant (HVS), Curbar Edge, Peak District*

pitches with one very hard move. Short pitches may take several minutes to climb, but most of this time is spent in resting or low-intensity work where the aerobic system can cope. ATP-PC would again be required for short bursts of hard moves. The situation may be rather different on sustained short pitches where even resting situations may be demanding more energy than the aerobic system can supply. Here the Lactic Acid system becomes the most important facet of performance.

*Long pitches*   These are much more likely to demand high levels of work for a couple of minutes or so, the Lactic Acid system being of most importance here. Although the pitch may take half an hour or so to climb, it is unlikely that the aerobic energy system will be of great significance. Most long pitches have a minute or two of movement with high energy output followed by periods of almost complete rest or quite low level work making little demand on the aerobic system − there are obviously exceptions to this generalisation.

From the above it would seem that the training emphasis should be on the anaerobic energy systems, especially the Lactic Acid system, with skill and strength becoming more important for the 'one move' situation. It would be unwise to ignore the aerobic energy system altogether though, for the more efficient the aerobic

system the higher the Anaerobic Threshold (the work rate at which the Lactic Acid system is switched on). A level of aerobic fitness would therefore conserve the limited LA-02 (Lactic Acid) energy supply. It would seem, though, that the traditional and effective aerobic training methods should not be prominent in a training programme. Better to use slightly less effective but more specific aerobic training exercises to increase aerobic performance.

A further complication in this understanding of energy systems and climbing performance is that much of the real difficulty and performance in movement emanates from a few quite small and highly specific finger muscles (contained in the forearm). The importance of 'energy systems fitness' may be over-emphasised; for these small muscles, increased performance capacity may be more dependent on changes taking place at the muscle such as increased muscle blood flow and capillary density. It is likely, however, that training the appropriate energy systems in a *specific* way will also be the best training to effect these muscular changes.

## TRAINING METHODS

There are numerous commonly used mediums for training; the best are outlined here in

approximate order of importance, with the best mentioned first. While the degree of specificity of the training medium is a very important factor in its value, real climbing situations are not ideal for the physical aspects of training. Effective training demands total preoccupation with the physical aspects of the exercise; this could well be dangerous in situations of real risk. Training mediums should

therefore be free of risk; the 'coping with danger' aspects of training should be practised separately.

## Climbing walls

Of all the facilities for climbing training, artificial climbing walls are by far the most useful. A good uncrowded, heated indoor wall is worth its weight in gold for climbing training. It is specific but can be used safely; it is heated, thereby increasing the comfort of the user and lessening the chance of injury. A good wall provides opportunity for a variety of training aims and also allows monitoring and progression.

A traverse at safe height should be the normal basis of LA-02 and aerobic training while a short 'circular' route provides a good ATP-PC training medium. Unfortunately, traversing is extravagant with wall space, so it is best to train when the wall is quiet, perhaps with a small group training together on a 'one way' traverse system.

Aerobic training on a wall is achieved by working the heart at between seventy and ninety per cent of its maximum pulse rate (H.R. max) – see table for an estimate. The heart rate should be maintained at this level for a total of thirty minutes or so per training session. This may be achieved by continuous work at the lower end of the training zone or interval work at the upper end; use both for variety and do not expect to work within the zone until fairly fit.

*Indoor climbing walls – a climber's most useful training facility*

*Maximum pulse rates and the training zone*

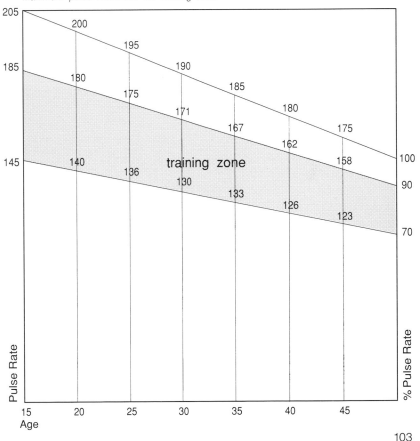

Intervals should be of 1:1 work/rest ratio with the work sessions lasting from four to ten minutes. Later the work/rest ratio should be improved to 2:1 with the same amount of H.R. recovery during rest as before. The actual work chosen on the wall is very important; it will be found that even seventy per cent H.R. max is impossible to achieve on difficult and fingery traverses. The traverse for aerobic training should be easy, with large holds, and ideally undulate along its length. It should be used both ways until the interval work period is complete and should work the legs, body and upper arms as much as possible. After a few sessions monitoring the heart rate it will be much easier (and quite accurate) to estimate the heart rate from the 'feel' of the work intensity on a stress scale. This avoids the hassle of H.R. monitoring during workouts. Progress is made first by cutting down recovery periods and then by measuring the number of traverses achieved in a given interval time at a given intensity of effort. However, aerobic training on a climbing wall is most difficult to organise and may need to be sought elsewhere; the next best option is circuit training.

Anaerobic training is what the climbing wall is all about; it is also the most important energy system in climbing performance. Again a traverse is ideal; it should be fingery and last between thirty seconds and two minutes. Work/rest ratios should start at 1:2

and improve to 2:1 fairly soon, while work intensity should be high, in the eighty to one hundred per cent range. This is LA-02 training and the number of reps will be limited initially by the forearms becoming 'pumped'. Active shaking out, or light work with the arms held low, speeds dissipation of the Lactic Acid

during the recovery period. Soon, however, a set of say 10 x 90 second reps will be possible. Later a second set may be added after a good rest period in which alternative exercise is done, say sets of high step-ups and sit-ups. Progress is best made after the initial breaking in period by increasing the difficulty (and hence

*Interval anaerobic training on Malham Cove, North Yorkshire: this climb takes about ninety seconds of sustained effort and is being done repeatedly on a top rope – Claudie Dunn training on Consenting Adults*

strenuousness) of the traverse.

ATP-PC training is best achieved with a short but very strenuous traverse lasting ten to twenty seconds, or better still a circular problem of four or five moves done on fingers alone with feet smearing. The work/rest ratio should be 1:4 or thereabouts with a maximum work intensity. Sets should consist of eight or ten reps with a rest of five to ten minutes between sets. Progress on a wall is best achieved by increasing the distance covered in a given time on each rep, thereby increasing intensity.

Strength training can be done on a climbing wall, but this would be a poor use of the facility; better to use weight training or a finger board.

## Bouldering

While climbing walls make excellent skill training facilities, real rock is better; though weather often dictates that the former is used. Bouldering as a form of training doesn't have to be on a boulder − any low level 'problem' work on climbing walls, boulders or real crags counts as bouldering. Skill training by bouldering normally incorporates some incidental strength training. Training is achieved by categorising climbing skills into areas such as mantelshelfing, laybacking aretes, edging, finger jamming or roofs, and pushing up

## Frequency

It is important to note two other important aspects of training: frequency and the warm-up/warm-down sessions. Most research indicates that quality rather than quantity is the key to effective training, and also that quality can only be achieved with proper rests between sessions. More than one session per day is likely to be counter-productive unless the second session is of a fundamentally different nature to the first. This is especially true after anaerobic or strength training sessions where in some cases the system may need more than twenty-four hours to recover.

The warm-up and warm-down are important aspects of training and climbing. The flexibility components of training can be incorporated into these sessions without impairing intensity of effort on the main session. A warm-up loosens and stretches muscles, connecting fibres and joints; it also prepares the energy systems and muscles for work, as muscular temperature is raised. All these factors increase preparedness for performance and reduce the chance of injury. Warm-downs speed recovery by maintaining blood circulation to remove waste products. Stretching here lengthens muscle fibres after shortening during strength training. A warm-up should consist of light appropriate muscular work that leaves one breathing more heavily than normal and feeling warm. It should also leave limbs and joints feeling mobile and free from stiffness.

one's ability in these categories by seeking harder examples of each. It is an interesting but somewhat surprising phenomenon that once an extremely difficult (for the individual) boulder problem is accomplished it can always be repeated with relative ease.

Style training is rather different from skill training in that one concentrates on overall efficiency of movement rather than desparate moves. Training is effected on sequences of moves of submaximal difficulty where you can concentrate on such aspects as keeping close to the rock or ensuring that the centre of gravity (C.G.) is brought over the support foot as soon as possible. If these skills are practised until they become autonomous, style will not desert the climber in situations of high drama and strength will be conserved.

## Circuit training

Circuit training does not have to be the traditional gymnasium-based exercise that most people are familiar with; indeed for climbing purposes it should not be. Circuits are simply sets of exercises that train, both aerobically and anaerobically, various specific muscles or groups of muscles used in climbing. Absolutely any activity can be included in a set of circuit situations, but all should be carefully assessed for specific type and relevance. Home-made circuits are easy to construct and may be sited indoors or out. Outdoor circuits can be particularly useful in that running can easily be incorporated into the circuit, giving a rest from the exercises relevant to the climber, which are predominantly based on the upper body. There is no need for each circuit station to be absolutely specific; general skeletal fitness is necessary as a base upon which the specific motions of the climber operate.

A circuit could have any number of stations, anything from five to twelve being usual, with care being exercised to separate activities on similar muscle groups. The circuit consists of visiting each station, performing a set of repetitions at each with no rest between stations. Subsequent circuits are made after a rest, two, three or four in total. The best way to set up and monitor a circuit is first to establish a repetition maximum for each activity; a typical session may then consist of a circuit at fifty per cent R.M. followed by circuits at seventy-five

per cent and one hundred per cent R.M. After every four weeks or so further monitoring sessions should establish new R.M.'s.

A set of typical and very specific exercises should include the following:

1  *Rope climbing* – up and down in control, hands only if possible.
2  *Bachar ladder* – hand over hand climbing up the underside of a ladder; the angle can be adjusted and feet can be used initially.
3  *Pull-ups* – use a bar with palms away from the face; keep in control up and down.
4  *Finger pull-ups* – a finger board is ideal for this, but a 1 cm wide piece of wood fastened to a bigger piece will do.
5  *Pinch-grip pull-ups* – use the ends of two 4 cm wide planks.
6  *Press-ups* – with fingers pointing towards each other to mimic mantelshelfs.
7  *Hand crack* – two 4 cm planks fastened together with a 4–6 cm 'crack' between (actual crack size depends on hand size). Like the Bachar ladder, this crack should be leant against a wall or suspended so that the angle can be adjusted from gently overhanging to roof.
8  *Sit-ups* – two types work different muscles; legs straight and not held or legs bent with toes held.

9  *Leg raises* – dead hang from bar then raise and lower legs towards the chest, keeping them straight.
10  *Squat jumps* – squat down then jump; try to use the toes as much as possible.
11  *Step-ups* – two kinds: Regular step-ups stepping on and off a 60–70 cm bench or equivalent. High step-ups are a slower, more strenuous version using a step at maximum height, usually about 1–1.20 m.
12  *Heel raises* – with toes only on a raised step, lower then raise the heels covering as large a range of movement as possible.

Runs of up to 800 metres can be interspersed between stations on outdor circuits, very nice in a Californian forest but a bit grim on some sleet-swept British moor. Note that the exercise should be made easier if the R.M. is below eight, but should be made more difficult, using weights if necessary, if the R.M.s get too large and lengthy.

## Flexibility

The importance of flexibility in climbing has gone unrecognised for too long. It should be an integral and substantial part of a training programme. Because flexibility training involves little in

Ron Fawcett on the superb last pitch of Triomphe D'Héros, Verdon Gorge, during its first free ascent

Martin Atkinson on To Bolt Or Not To Be, Smith Rock, Oregon

*Ron Fawcett spacewalking on the second pitch of Pichenibule, Verdon Gorge, France, during its first ascent*

the way of muscular exertion or energy system stress, it is an ideal training medium to be coupled with muscular work during warm-up, warm-down, and rest intervals.

The key areas to work on for climbing are the hip and hamstring, which govern the movement of the spine and trunk, followed by shoulder, abdomen and lower leg work. As people lose flexibility with age and with muscle development, it is necessary for the training climber to be engaged in stretching exercises just to avoid deteriorioration; but extra work on top of this can have a dramatic effect on climbing performance and enjoyment, especially for those who see themselves as lacking mobility.

There are three distinct methods of increasing mobility, involving different ways of stretching. *Passive stretching* is safest and most readily usable to every one. This involves pressing the limb or joint system to be stretched to its maximum extension position in the desired direction, using the antagonist muscles (those which enable the limb to return to a straight position) alone. The position should be held for thirty seconds. There should be no 'bouncing' of the limbs to achieve greater stretch, merely a steady muscular contraction of the antagonist muscles. Successive exercises should alternate different muscle groups or areas of the body.

*Active* or *dynamic stretching*

methods involve bouncing the limb, using its own weight or the body weight for momentum. This method is not to be recommended due to the high risk of damage or injury to the muscles, tendons or connective tissues involved.

The third stretching method is more effective than passive stretching and safer than dynamic stretching; it should, however, be done thoughtfully and with careful planning. *P.N.F.* (*Proprioceptive Neuromuscular Facilitation*) is an active stretching technique that simply fools or conditions the stretch inhibitor Golgi receptors in the tendons, allowing greater movement in that muscular system. (Receptors are a type of nerve ending sited in various body tissues which transmit messages back to the brain on the condition of that part of the body.) P.N.F. stretching involves passive movement of the limb to the limit of its range. A partner then *holds* (not pushes) the limb steadily in that position while the subject presses hard against the holder in an effort to straighten the limb (i.e. bring it back to its central position). The effort is maintained for five seconds after which both helper and subject relax slowly and in co-ordination. The subject then passively stretches the same limb to its new limit. If a partner is not available it is possible by careful manoeuvring to get a solid surface such as the wall or floor to act as the partner. It is important to stress that the limb does isometric work

only during the pressing stage, i.e. no limb movement is involved.

While a wide range of stretching exercises should be used to maintain an overall level of flexibility, a base to complement general muscular fitness, certain exercises are key elements of climbing performance.

1   *Inner thigh stretch* – legs at right angles to the trunk are pressed apart.
2   *Splits* – one leg is fully extended forwards, the other backwards with the trunk upright.
3   *Hips and hamstrings 1* – sit upright with legs as wide apart as possible and hands together stretched above the head. Lean over to touch each toe in turn.
4   *Hips and hamstrings 2* – trail one leg straight out behind and squat on front leg, getting hips as low as possible.
5   *Hips and hamstrings 3* – kneel on rear leg, front leg out straight in front. Bend over forwards, keeping back straight and arms straight by the side.
6   *Hips and hamstrings 4* – touch alternate toes with both hands; legs apart.
7   *Side bends* – stand upright with one arm extended above the head. The other arm slides down the leg with the spine bending sideways.
8   *Shoulders 1* – bend over in front of a bench with arms

stretched upwards so that the palms rest on the bench. Press the head and shoulders down.

9 *Shoulders 2* – using a piece of rope or rod (a broom handle would do), grip with outstretched arms and circle both arms above the head until the arms point backwards. The arms have to be wide apart initially, being brought closer as flexibility improves.

## Weight training

Weight training is the best way of gaining strength for climbing; in other spheres of training different media are more suitable. Generally speaking, a gain in strength is achieved by working on sets containing low numbers of reps with high loads. Pyramid sets are effective strength trainers which build up to your maximum load in steps with decreasing numbers of reps. First you should establish your maximum load at any particular exercise. A set would then consist of:

10 reps at 75%.
 8 reps at 80%.
 6 reps at 85%.
 4 reps at 90%.
 2 reps at 95%.

or something similar. Monitoring takes place after two or three weeks when new maximum loads are established and progress is recorded. The exercises suggested here are specific and are listed in approximate order of usefulness:

1 *Chins or pull-ups* (with weight belt) – have one hundred per cent as maximum load with weights, but seventy-five per cent should be body only. Hands should be wide apart for one set and close for another and palms should also alternate; facing or facing away.
2 *Leg press* (using a Multigym) – best to use one leg at a time, this is more like the real thing and allows you to monitor each leg independently. It also stops one leg doing all the work.
3 *Bench press* – use a narrow grip in preference to a wide one, though some alternating is useful.
4 *Rows* – should be done both with hands over the bar and under.
5 *Toe press* – use the leg press site and keep the legs straight with toes only on the press paddle. Move the foot through as large a range of movement as possible.
6 *Pinch grips* – use a smooth-sided plate weight if possible and raise to the waist and lower.
7 *Body curls* – on an inclined bench with feet held, the steeper the incline the harder; can be done with a weight held behind the head.

There are of course many other exercises which aid other aspects of muscular development. Some of them should be incorporated into a minor, less frequent, programme so that the musculature in general is strengthened.

## TRAINING REGIMES

A training regime is built up from the components previously described. The emphasis should reflect the needs (weaknesses) of the individual while bearing in mind the demands of the type of climbing being trained for:

Bouldering –
    strength predominant
Multi-pitch limestone –
    aerobic and anaerobic mix
Steep single-pitch –
    strength and anerobic
General crag climbing –
    anaerobic predominant

Each training session should include a flexibility component lasting ten minutes or so. In all training, quality should be emphasised before quantity and rest periods are very important. For this reason climbers should train no more than once a day, and sessions need last no more than one hour rising to two hours for top-level performers. There should probably be three phases to a year:

1 A *rest phase* of about two months where training is light

and done every other day. This period follows the main climbing/competition season.

2 A *main training phase* where much of the building work is done. This phase should last between four and six months, depending on the length of the main season, and training should take place daily.

3 The *main climbing season phase*, in which the training should be structured around the climbing itself so that any 'building' work or high-intensity training takes place soon after the actual climbing. During the rest of the week (or training cycle) the intensity drops off to a rest day before the next climbing session(s).

Note that grouping together hard strength or anaerobic sessions may be counter-productive – allow forty-eight hours between such sessions unless you are sure that you are recovering sufficiently in twenty-four hours.

The yearly programme is of course approximate and should be tailored to individual needs. A climber training for competitions, for instance, may find that the season lasts twelve months but with a week or two for 'building' work after each competition. There should always be a tail-off in activity intensity, especially strength and anaerobic work, before a competition.

## MENTAL TRAINING

Many of the traditional psychological features of climbing encountered by virtue of exposure, poor protection, serious routes and the like are disappearing on modern bolt-protected routes. Instead we shall have the purely physical gymnastic skills favoured by the bolting boulderers. This lament aside, it must be said that the vast majority of climbing is still about the combination of a natural physical activity and a series of mental problems in the shape of calculating risks, overcoming fear, concentrating, motivating oneself to continue and dealing with the problem-solving demands of the route itself. There is much activity in terms of training and fitness for climbing these days, but virtually all the focus is on the physiological aspects of fitness while the psychological is virtually ignored. Are we to infer from this that it is of much less significance in performance? I think not. It is, however, less tangible than the physical, and it is less easy to visualise how you can train for it; it lacks the satisfying feeling of 'being pumped' after a workout and there are no shiny rippling bundles of muscles to show for it.

However, most people know some climbers, strong fit specimens, who consistently fail to perform away from the safe confines of the bottom three metres of the climbing wall; and

there are those who avoid leading like the plague, but can second absolutely anything. There are also those many climbers, leaders or seconds, whose performance drops remarkably when transferring from outcrops to mountain crags or 400 m alpine limestone faces. Experienced climbers can usually cite extreme examples of such behaviour, but the fact is that this phenomenon affects us all to some degree or other, though it may be difficult to measure. It also affects climbers at all levels and at all stages of experience, whereas the physical regimes of training at present being developed are more appropriate to routes of higher standard only.

There are three major aspects of the psychological in climbing performance: the development of skills, which is dealt with elsewhere in this book; the enhancement and control of motivation, which is the favourite of coaches in sport generally, but perhaps not so appropriate for the inherently individualistic nature of climbing; and finally there is the area of greatest importance to climbers, the emotional – for it is here that great climbing potential is lost rather than gained and much that is enjoyable also disappears.

Emotion has many facets, all of which may play a part in climbing performance – pleasure, unhappiness, aggression and so on. As far as the functioning of the body is concerned they are all pretty much the same thing – they cause the body to operate in a state of heightened arousal. Through our understanding of the situation we also know whether the experience is good and to be pursued or bad and to be avoided. While the emotions mentioned above are present in climbing, it is in that emotion characterised by feelings of apprehension, anxiety, fear or terror that the greatest effects on climbing performance are to be found.

The process is reasonably simple and fairly well understood. The climber confronts an external threat – it could be the height and exposure, the relative difficulty, lack of protection, risk of a painful fall, loose rock, being committed if one continues and so on; in fact climbing is all about meeting this external threat. A new threat has surfaced recently, as one or two top climbers have found to their cost – the threat posed by the need to perform and compete in front of an audience. Some just cannot handle that situation while others appear to thrive on it. Added to the external threat is the individual's propensity towards anxiousness – a deep-seated trait that differs between individuals and influences one's reaction to a threat. The result is a feeling of anxiety and its accompanying physiological component of stress, or more accurately arousal. The degree of stress is related to the size of imbalance perceived between the threat and one's

ability to meet it.

The effect on performance varies from the subtle to the dramatic and can be positive as well as negative; some apprehension and subsequent arousal can be the incentive to fight your way up a brutish overhanging crack. More often we experience difficulty in concentrating on the task – our thoughts switch to the threat and ways of avoiding it. Some climbers begin to shake, some talk loudly, seeking the support of others, some freeze and are unable to operate; but perhaps the vast majority of experienced climbers just 'give the route best' and retreat in a greater or lesser disarray. Lots of irrational behaviour occurs in these situations, such as the 'drowning man grasps at straws' syndrome when climbers make ridiculous 'scrabbling' moves that are totally without their usual skills or throw in useless protection, then grab it.

While it is easy to see that anxiety effects performance, it is difficult to quantify its influence on climbing performance as a whole, mainly because climbing performance itself is such a slippery quantity. Perhaps the best attempts at analysing the effects of anxiety and stress have involved the measurement of a 'performance decrement' – in climbing, a rough measurement of the difference between climbing performance in a 'safe' environment (e.g. a climbing wall,

top-rope route or seconding) and performance when leading on the crag. The size of the performance decrement varies widely between individuals but, strangely, seems to be only loosely related to the amount of anxiety experienced by an individual in climbing situations. Even less relationship is noticed between a person's innate propensity to be anxious, a personality trait, and climbing performance.

This relationship between lack of anxiety/stress and performance is most interesting and fruitful in discovering ways of eliminating performance decrement in threatening situations (though it should be mentioned that to overcome the effects of anxiety completely may not be desirable, for some anxiety serves to alert us to the very real dangers of some climbing situations). How does that relationship between anxiety and climbing performance work, and what can we do about it?

There exists a beautiful slim face climb on Bosigran's Great Zawn in Cornwall called Déja Vu. During an early ascent I wondered how the name arose; one leaves the Green Cormorant Lodge via a series of unprotected but reasonable moves, then follow a gradually diminishing line of holds up a thin slab, still with no protection. At some point on this thin face one realises that retreat may be impossible, that above looks blank and there is no protection below for ten metres or so. Legs begin to quiver, thoughts of the lack of protection and the possible fall take over and the reason for the name becomes apparent − how often do climbers find themselves in that situation? The solution is obvious; carry on climbing or try and get down − but either is usually accomplished with far less skill than one normally possesses.

The Inverted 'U' Theory or Yerkes-Dodson Law (not a law at all) partially describes what has happened: an increase in anxiety and stress causes increased arousal of our bodies' activating systems and we are sharpened up for the climbing − we perform better. This happens early on in the example above. At some stage, however, the anxiety increases and the consequent arousal becomes a hindrance to performance rather than a help; performance from there on begins to deteriorate. While the novice allows performance to deteriorate to zero, i.e. he freezes or leaps for a passing seagull, the more experienced climber manages to focus on the solution and control the arousal overload to enable protection to be reached. Once reached, of course, anxiety and arousal drop dramatically.

As arousal increases after protection is left the focus of one's attention narrows − which is fine so long as it is the task of climbing that attention is focused upon. All extraneous information is cut out and all concentration is on the skill of climbing. As anxiety increases,

however, two things may happen − attentional focus may narrow further and begin to cut out some of the information necessary for the accomplishment of the climb, or we may experience an attentional switch where the object of our attentional focus switches from climbing to our mounting anxiety, getting down or to safety or even our position and the drop.

There are various sorts of mental training one can do before climbing that will improve confidence and limit the distracting effects of anxiety. Most of these techniques centre on some sort of goal setting or visualisation exercise. In climbing it is most likely that this 'pre-climb' work will take place some hours before the climbing session, or the day before. In a more general sense, one can set goals for a climbing season or a trip abroad. It is important to set realistic goals; if you are a 3c climber it is of little use deciding your goal is to be 7c. Set goals in small stages so that you quickly acquire the confidence that you will succeed in attaining the goal. It will also be easier because you are more familiar with the territory: a 3c leader knows what 4b routes are like and can visualise the skills required to climb them. It is also an important point not to think of a 'goal' merely in terms of '4b' but of the process by which one climbs a 4b route − the extra skill or strength, for instance, that you will display. Better still, visualise an actual route (from

looking at it, the guidebook description, photographs etc.); be specific about what aspect of the route will test your skill. But remember that it is no use visualising yourself creaming perfectly up a 4b layback if you don't know what it feels like to be on a 4b layback − you must have some basis for visualisation. That basis would normally come from experiencing the same movement in a lesser 'climbing game'; for instance, the crag climber would experience 4b laybacks in the safety and comfort of a climbing wall − the sense of 'perfect movement' could then be visualised in the more daunting crag situation. Similarly, a climber about to do a big wall route can treat each pitch as a separate goal and relate the technical difficulty to some movement experience on single-pitch routes.

It is very important that this mental rehearsal should evoke feelings of pleasure, enjoyment and success. If you evoke feelings of boredom, frustration or anxiety when you visualise, then forget it and try something different. It can be a help in visualisation to replace your own experience with that of an ideal model. You may struggle with little skill and much effort up a finger-jamming crack, so watch someone do it perfectly, analyse what they are doing and what the fundamentals of their skill are; visualise yourself doing the crack with that ideal skill. You have to try to feel yourself doing it, feel what it is like to be laying sideways off a finger jam with weight off-loaded onto a marginal foothold – feel it working.

There are, then, three things that we should try to control; anxiety, attentional narrowing and attentional switching. With all these phenomena half the battle in controlling them is won by understanding what they are and how they function. The latter two are particularly easy to control and work with – just practise (on the climbing wall perhaps, or bouldering) deliberately switching attention to the drop, or broken legs, then switching back again to the skill of climbing beautifully. I use the phrase 'skill of climbing beautifully' deliberately – for me it has always been a better notion to focus on than say 'reaching the resting spot', because the former requires efficient climbing of the sort most likely to succeed whereas the latter may induce an undignified scrabble that is more likely to result in a fall. It is important to remember that the cues or task you focus on should be well-learnt and familiar – unwanted attentional switching occurs much more readily if the task you are trying to attend to is one which itself raises doubts about your ability to cope.

The solution in this example, and for other phenomena, is one of concentration on the task of climbing. This can be achieved in a variety of ways, but perhaps the two most successful are to think

through or mentally rehearse the skilled components of a crucial route the night before, and on the route itself to think only of skill and style in relation to any one section of climbing. The former technique displaces anxiety to the evening before and builds confidence on the route itself as the elements of the rehearsal are 'ticked off' successfully. The latter technique is a deliberate attempt to fill all thinking capacity with skill-related issues and thus to eliminate the intrusion of unwanted information such as thinking about the threat.

Attentional width can be controlled in the same way. While climbing or training deliberately 'focus down' to something quite specific, then widen your attention so that you are utilising a predetermined set of environmental cues. When real anxiety-provoking situations cause attentional narrowing – the 'tunnel vision' of learner drivers – you are then prepared with the response, a set of necessary cues that must not be cut out. They may be things such as the technicalities of the move ahead, scanning the rock for protection or moving with fluency and efficiency.

Anxiety itself is a little more difficult to control, but again it helps if it can be excluded from the attentional span by focusing on the skill in hand. There are, however, two techniques or phenomena which help to remove the anxiousness itself: displacement and habituation. Researchers have

found that novice sky divers were most anxious just before they leapt out of the plane, but experienced jumpers, although showing similar levels of anxiousness, peaked in anxiety the evening before the jump. In other words, they had thought through the experience the evening before, becoming anxious at a time when it could not affect the physical performance itself. It is possible, therefore, to displace anxiety to a time when it will not disturb the climbing itself – the evening before an important and difficult route you can think through the route and all the difficulties it may present and experience the sweaty palms, but at the same time rationalise that you are able to climb the route any way, and could therefore do it solo if necessary. By morning you are already committed to the route and further anxiety is neither necessary or relevant.

Habituation is a rather different idea, but it centres on two separate notions. First, it is possible to reduce the amount of arousal generated by becoming familiar with the cause of stress – the 'familiarity breeds contempt' notion. The novice is anxious because of things like heights; this cause of arousal is reduced by spending lots of time in 'height situations', not necessarily while climbing. If the fear of falling is a problem, get on a route above some safe protection and leap off a few times, or jump off a bridge or two with a climbing rope tied to the parapet — check the length carefully! In that way you become accustomed to the source of stress so that it is no longer a threat. Of course, if it's broken legs you're frightened of you have a problem! It is also possible to habituate to stress itself, just by getting used to operating in situations of higher stress than you would normally like — but remember that stress is probably a specific phenomenon and that habituating to the stress of say, public speaking, will not help in a situation of stress caused by the fear of physical injury or falling. The habituating therefore needs to be with the specific causes of stress found in climbing.

It is important when developing anxiety-reducing strategies to recognise in advance what situations or parts of a climb are likely to produce anxiety. You can then have specific methods, tried and tested, to deal with such situations. The methods described above have worked for me in the climbing situation, but they may not be for everyone. People do need different tactics and situations to reduce anxiety and cope with the climb, as can frequently be seen in the ways in which individual climbers react to the presence of others. Some climbers need quiet and lack of contact with others both before and during a climb; others require social interaction and reinforcement at all times, often keeping up an incessant babble of conversation and repartee during a climb.

Other related techniques that may help include the rehearsal techniques mentioned earlier. At a resting spot below the crux or a bold section, rehearse the movement skills to follow and grow safe in the knowledge that you are about to execute the moves perfectly. A variation of this would be to visualise youself possessing a particular quality crucial to the section ahead. For instance, internalise a feeling of great strength, balance or dynamism if one of these qualities is a key to the climbing ahead. Remembering positive key words or phrases learnt during pre-climbing visualisation serves to occupy the mind with positive high-quality attributes and skills.

If overtaken by anxiety most climbers will find some kind of quiet thought technique useful in order to calm down before concentrating on pure climbing skills. Looking intently at something unusual and close to hand might work; staring at the crystals and colours on a minute piece of rock a few centimetres in front of your eyes will aid relaxation. At the same time breathe slowly and deeply, concentrating on letting the breath out slowly. You do of course need a resting place or relatively safe spot to engage in this technique — a high degree of 'holding on' effort from the arms will probably make it impossible to concentrate on some 'off the job' relaxation feature.

Another technique which has been used by some climbers, though personally I have not found it helpful, is to imagine you are something, or somebody, else before a particularly difficult section. For instance, a particularly daunting stretch of hauling up overhangs on widely spaced jugs could be dealt with by imagining you are about to climb it 'as if I am an ape' or whatever other 'as if' imagery seems suitable.

With practical mastery of these coping techniques and fine judgement of your own technical ability, there should be no reson why your climbing wall or top-rope standard should not be matched by your leading standard.

# 12  *Advanced techniques*

As climbs get difficult the climber develops the techniques to meet the increased difficulty. For many aspects of climbing on difficult ground this merely means doing more difficult versions of the original skill; laybacking, for instance, will be the same movement, but the crack for the hands may be fingertip size or have a rounded edge and be steep. No special extra skill is required, though, just a high degree of proficiency at the basic movement.

The special problems of difficult climbs are not therefore concerned with standard techniques but with such aspects as steepness, continuous difficulty or tiny holds. Here new problems and solutions have to be solved to make progress possible. Perhaps the most important single feature about hard routes is that pitches tend to be continuously difficult or steep, and actually holding on becomes a problem. The first resting place after the start of the pitch is frequently the stance at the end of the pitch. It rapidly becomes obvious to any climber that the fingers are not strong enough to hold on to small holds for more than a few minutes without help. The key to overcoming this sort of problem

lies in two techniques; one is to help the fingers and arms as much as possible with other stronger muscles, and the other is simply training for more finger stamina. Training has already been discussed in chapter 11; here we are concerned with relieving the fingers by more efficient movement.

## EFFICIENT MOVEMENT

Efficient movement is really about two things: clever use of balance when progressing upwards, and clever use of balance and holds when stationary to relieve weaker muscles. There is a misconception among non-climbers (and probably many climbers too) that balance in climbing is about the ability to walk a tightrope or stand on one foot on top of a pointed rock. These kinds of balance are all about a narrow base and a high centre of gravity (C.G.) being kept above that base by the body's balance sensors warning of impending imbalance. In climbing we have a narrow base, but balance is kept by a hand or two gently pushing the body over the centre of gravity. When stepping up on a new foothold the hands

keep the centre of gravity over its new base as the leg pushes up the whole body. The clever use of this latter form of balancing is the technical key to efficient movement.

The game is to get up a steep sustained pitch by doing as little work as possible with the weakest muscles, which are those controlling the fingers and hand (in the forearm), and those controlling the lower arm (biceps) and upper arm (shoulder and back). The muscles to use instead are the thigh and upper and lower leg muscles. On walls of any steepness one does this by positioning the centre of gravity (a point in the lower abdomen in most people) as near as possible to some point over the base. The base will normally be one foot or the other, or between both feet. It is important to realise that even if both feet are on holds this position may not permit the C.G. to be positioned above the base; it is therefore necessary to use the best of the two feet as the only base. On climbs up to and including the vertical the hands and fingers need only be used in a very gentle fashion to lightly position the C.G. over a base. The base can be effectively moved out away from the rock to aid this balance by choosing two footholds with a concave rock shape between (bridging in effect) and by making sure the heels are locked at right sure the heels are locked at right angles and pointing straight out from the rock. On overhanging rock, and in the absence of a suitable bridging position, it is simply a question of pressing the body against the rock to keep the discrepancy between base and C.G. as low as possible. Every centimetre the C.G. is brought closer to the base will shed kilogrammes from the finger load.

In moving upwards the base over which the C.G. is balanced will change. Less able climbers tend to haul their body weight from one to the other with fingers and hands. An efficient technique requires that the lead foot be moved up and the C.G. be positioned over the new base, if possible before any upward movement of the body has taken place. Once positioned the bent leg supporting the body above the base can be straightened, again using very small positioning effort from the fingers and hands. It is frequently not possible to get the C.G. above the base before moving, so that the idea must be to get it there are soon as possible after the move has started. This is often best achieved by a dynamic movement of the body to its new position. In this case this is

achieved by a slight recoil movement, then a sharp upward movement using arm pulling and trail foot pushing simultaneously. This should produce enough momentum for the C.G. to settle with little further effort over the new base.

Speed of movement can be an important factor in efficiency for two reasons. First and most simply, the faster one climbs a pitch or goes between resting places the less time one spends hanging at least part of the body weight on fingers. Second, to conserve

*Climbing steep rock on tiny holds — hurry up or fall off*

upward momentum is much more efficient in energy conservation terms than a 'stop-start' sort of progress. This is especially true on some friction climbs when upward momentum allows a foothold to be useful in aiding movement: to stop the same foothold might result in the foot slipping off because of the increased downward pressure on the hold. Accomplished climbers will use a resting place to work out as many moves above as possible, or will use it as a haven to retreat to after working out a couple of moves above. A further foray or two will enable more moves above to be worked out until the next rest can be reached.

Exactly how a climber uses the weaker hands and arms is important. Try two ways of holding on to a pull-up bar, either a dead hang with the arms straight or with the elbows locked at right angles: invariably the former position allows you to hold on for much longer. Limbs do less work if they are extended, so try to use them in this position. Leaning sideways on a steep wall from a side-hold is much more efficient and relaxing than hanging with bent arm from a hold above.

## Bridging

We have seen that bridging techniques hold the climber in position in corners and grooves by allowing the C.G. to lie between the two outstretched legs (the base) and the rock itself. In this position the hands can be taken off the rock completely. On steep or overhanging walls bridging can be used to improve the efficiency of movement and resting by taking load from the arms; it can also be used to create footholds where there appear to be none. On a steep wall, two inward-facing side holds can be used for the feet to press on in a bridged position. The pressing action to keep the feet in place also allows the legs to be used to press the body in towards the rock, thus taking much of the load from the arms.

## Locking off

On very steep rock where the fingers and arms are used a great deal for the upward movement itself, the climber will sooner or later come upon a move which he does not possess the sheer arm or finger strength to make. This normally occurs during upward movement where it is necessary both to move up and take one hand off to reach a higher hold. It is the one arm pull-up situation that defeats the climber. In most circumstances, however, this move can be avoided by pulling up as far as possible on both arms until the trailing arm is bent at its most powerful holding position, i.e. at right angles or fully bent. The limb is then 'locked' still while the other arm is carefully moved up to the new hold. Jerky movement or lunges cause unnecessary load on the locked arm and should be avoided.

## Resting

We have already seen how careful manipulation of the C.G. and steep wall-bridging techniques can be used to rest on hard or steep climbs. The importance of resting is that it gives the arm and finger muscles chance to recover. Most steep climbing armwork uses the Lactic Acid energy system which registers fatigue by a build-up of the lactic acid waste product in the muscle. The muscle (usually the forearm) becomes hard and unable to perform any work; it is said to be 'pumped'. A substantial amount of the lactic acid can be removed by resting the limb, or better still by lowering then shaking the limb gently. This promotes circulation and speeds recovery. After a couple of minutes of 'shaking out' further progress is usually possible. Resting, then, can be of individual limbs as they are shaken out; other limbs may not actually be 'resting' while this is going on, though of course the less work they are doing the better.

In order to rest the arms properly they both need to be off the rock and hanging down. This is simple enough on a ledge and is not too difficult to do from a bridging position; balance is retained by leaning inwards and resting head, shoulders or upper body on the rock for stability. Other resting possibilities involve bridging with one or two feet and another part of the anatomy, say knee, thigh, body or shoulders. Again a stable position is maintained and the arms can be shaken out.

*Locks* are an extension of jamming techniques whereby the length of any one section of a limb is wedged across a crack or hole in the rock, so holding the body in one place with very little muscular effort. Although locks are used for progress on big roofs and overhangs they are of most use in resting – especially if the leg is doing the locking. Perhaps the most efficient and impressive lock is the knee lock or knee bar. Imagine a rounded hole on the underside of a roof, a feature frequently found on steep limestone, that is some fifty to sixty centimetres in diameter. While hanging ape-like from the edge of the hole (or adjacent holds), the lower leg is brought up and wedged across the hole with the foot on one side and the knee on the other. It is then possible to let go with the hands and hang upside down from the roof to shake out. There are of course lots of less dramatic knee bar rests around, but the example is a good one. Heel and toe locks are encountered quite frequently, while a body lock, or rather body jam, can be used to effect in

*A leg hook and toe lock combination*

narrow chimneys or wide cracks simply by twisting the body crossways in the chimney and so wedging the body.

Narrowings in fist- or off-width cracks frequently provide 'hands off' rests if the lower leg can be slid into the crack so that it jams on the wide part at the knee or mid-thigh. Large roofs often have wide horizontal cracks or flakes running beneath them; here the climber can hang upside down with the lower portion of both legs resting in the horizontal crack — a very relaxing position.

## TINY OR POOR HOLDS

Typical characteristics of hard routes are small holds, poor holds and holds with great blank gaps between them. Extra expertise is needed to cope successfully with climbs containing such problems.

### Tiny holds

These are obviously in the eye of the beholder; the beginner labels quite substantial jugs as tiny, while today's leading climbers would classify 1 or 2 mm flakes on slabs or 3–4 mm edges on walls as tiny. To get the most benefit from holds such as these it is necessary to use fingertips on the holds with the last segment of the finger pointing vertically downwards so that the fingernails are against the rock. The fingers are aided in this curled position by bending the thumb over the first joint of the forefinger. Such holds are painful for the fingertips until the tips become hardened by training in similar positions. Remember that the art of using such small holds successfully lies not in taking the full body weight on a knife-blade-sized flake but in making sure that very little of the body weight needs to be taken on the hold. A tiny hold may only be good for a pull of say one quarter of the body weight, but may nevertheless be crucial to accomplishing the move.

On limestone and some sandstones tiny holes taking just one or two fingers are common. Here it is a good idea to 'stack' the wider middle finger over the forefinger for extra support as well as using the thumb in the way described above. Small fingertip holes with sharp edges and fingertip widenings in hairline cracks can be used quite effectively by relaxing the fingers to a large extent. Here much of the weight is held by a combination of friction and jamming of the finger ends rather than the small groups of muscles controlling the last segment of the fingers.

For the feet to use tiny holds effectively the boot edge must be in good condition and be fairly hard and stiff. The feet are splayed outwards so that the whole length alongside the big toe can be carefully placed on the hold.

Conversely, pocket holds can only be used by the boot tips; they are very difficult to use with highly flexible boots, but stiffened insoles in flexible boots will make all the difference.

### Poor holds

These are holds that are either sloping and rounded or are facing the wrong way for use in the particular situation. Sloping and rounded holds are dealt with partly by making sure that a large area of well-chalked fingers is in contact with the hold (a good alternative to chalk in these situations is Tincture of Benzoine — Friar's Balsam — but this needs to be applied before the pitch is started). In addition to increasing friction, the way in which the hold is used becomes important: the pull exerted on the hold must be maintained in the optimum direction. For instance, if you are to pull up on a sloping hold the forearm would be held vertical and close to the rock to eliminate the tendency to pull outwards. As the move progresses this natural tendency to allow the forearm to move out and up must be resisted and its position maintained. Similarly, with holds that slope or face in awkward directions the fingers and forearm are placed in the best position possible and the move carried out by allowing the rest of the body to rotate around the fixed forearm. Again, allowing the forearm or hand to move will

break the friction contact and reduce its subsequent value.

Good footwork on poor holds again relies on as much of the sole as possible remaining in contact with the rock. Flexible high friction soles and the ability to angle the foot to get the optimum position are the keys to achieving good contact.

## Hooks

Hooks are really good holds used by poor parts of the body. The most common hooks are toe and heel hooks and the most common use is in taking part of the body weight when hanging under roofs. Pockets or holes on severely overhanging rock can be utilised by hooking the back of the heel or the toe over the lip of the hole and curling the body slightly so that hands and feet are pulling against each other. This makes the hook secure and has the effect of sharing the load between hands and feet. Another good use for a hook is found in pulling over the lip of a roof. Here the hands must be unloaded as much as possible, and a heel hook over the lip of the roof level with − or even above − the hands will do the trick. As height is gained the heel hook foot rolls over to become a high foothold which can be 'rolled over' until the body weight is over the foot.

## Widely spaced holds

These are tackled in a variety of ways but most common is the use of the undercling. All kinds of useless ripples on the rock turn into excellent underclings if the body is high enough in relation to a hold. Underclings allow the lead arm to go up at full stretch for a distant hold and as the stretch gets higher so the undercling hold feels better. A favourite trick on steep walls is to do half a move on a conventional handhold, until this begins to lose effectiveness, then find a very poor intermediate hold for the lead hand. This poor hold should be just sufficient to hold the body in place so that the trail hand can be switched from its conventional hold to some adjacent undercling. The move is then completed by the lead hand.

In the absence of the underclings the conventional handhold must be used to gain as much height as possible. This could be done by turning the handhold into a mantelshelf as you move up. Fifteen centimetres or so more height can be gained with good jug holds by leaving the fingers behind the tip of the jug as you move up, so that in the final stages of the move the trail hand is pointing vertically downwards with palm pressing outwards against the lip. This holds the body against the rock as the feet press the body upwards to gain height.

## LEVITATION

This section is devoted to the 'state of the art' tricks at present being employed or envisaged by climbers extending the boundaries of technique.

*Dynos* are 'dynamic' moves employed to cross pieces of rock between handholds that are too far apart for the techniques in the previous section to be of use. Dynos rely on a good push from the feet to propel the climber and his lead hand up a piece of rock to a hold that could not be reached solely by use of the trail hand's hold. Failure to reach the destination hold results in a fall or sometimes recovering on the lower hand hold. The technique is obviously best practised on a climbing wall where it will be found that success depends upon just the right amount of momentum being imparted to the body by the spring of the feet. The idea is to just reach the hold comfortably so that there is no upward or downward movement of the body as the hold is grasped. As an aid to stabilising oneself at the end of the lunge the rock is slapped with the lead hand. This stops movement and creates some friction so that the hold itself can be located securely. Sometimes a series of slaps are made as successive dynamic pushes are made towards the hold in question.

*Second Dyn dynos* involve the trail hand actually leaving the last handhold so that the body is in full flight between holds. Careful aim and accurate flight paths with the correct momentum are obviously crucial here. *Third Dyn* flights involve prolonging the flight by using a poor intermediate hold to maintain momentum for a great distance. These moves are at present being practised by dyno experts such as Johnny Dawes. Only the author has so far reached the *Fifth Dyn,* where entire short routes are climbed by a dyno originating on the ground and using several poor intermediate holds to maintain momentum. This technique has been tuned to full perfection in the author's mind.

*Crossovers* are real party tricks that actually work quite well. They can be used as an alternative to dynos, but work best where dynos are difficult to execute properly, i.e. when there are no footholds for a good take-off or when the target hold is very poor. A crossover needs a reasonably positive hand or finger hold, preferably an incut of some kind. From a hanging position on the left hand (if the right hand is to be the lead hand), with extra help from the right hand on the same hold if necessary, run the feet up the wall, then bend the right leg up high and pass the right

*Steve Rhodes attempting a crossover at Almscliff – with more flexibility he might manage it!*

Doing interval training using a self-top-roping system: a tape chest harness helps the prussik device slide up the rope foot over the left wrist. Allow the right thigh to come to rest on the wrist close to the knee. As the thigh is settled onto the wrist the wrist should be angled upwards so that maximum height is achieved. From this stable sitting position the right hand can reach without hurry for the next hold. This technique gains thirty to forty centimetres more height than would be attainable using standard techniques in the same circumstances, though not quite as much as a mantelshelf would gain from a protruding hold.

# 13 *Competition climbing*

Amid scenes of great debate and controversy, competition climbing has arrived on the traditionally unstructured climbing scene and it is here to stay. As yet it only directly involves the top five or ten per cent of climbers, most of whom make, or would like to make, some money out of climbing. It should be pointed out, of course, that most of those who wish to make money only do so in order to finance their full-time training and climbing regimes. There is, however, a growing professionalism in rock climbing, and this, coupled with an expansion of the competition systems to regional and local level, means that more and more climbers will become involved and also seek to make a living from climbing. Money at present comes from sponsorship by the climbing equipment manufacturers; as more people become involved in the competition scene, so more sponsorship money will become available.

There are two essentially different styles of climbing competition: speed competitions and difficulty competitions. Speed climbing was first on the scene, having evolved in Russia and other Eastern European nations. The idea is to climb a route, top-roped, as fast as possible. Difficulty competitions, on the other hand, involve eliminator competitions on routes of increasing difficulty, the highest point reached on a competitor's final route being the score. Most competitions these days take place on artificial indoor walls though there are still some outdoor competitions, mostly for speed climbing. One of the great problems in devising competitions is that the routes must be 'new' to all competitors; this means building an artificial wall or creating a new route by altering natural rock. This latter option is environmentally unacceptable in most countries and is certainly contrary to the spirit of the organising body, the U.I.A.A. So outdoor competitions will probably be limited in future to new crags that have not been climbed before; these are only really suitable for speed climbing, where several routes of carefully graduated difficulty are not required.

Internationally, competitions are governed by the C.E.C. (Climbing Competitions Committee) of the U.I.A.A. This body has a sub-committee, the Comité Internationale de Compétitions d'Escalade (C.I.C.E.) which is responsible for the actual structure and running of competitions (juries, judges, rules etc.). A series of international competitions, Grands Prix, are held at intervals each year in a variety of countries. These competitions have prizes provided by local sponsors and also enable competitors to gain points towards a Grand Prix Final. In addition many of the Grand Prix competitions will double as the National Championship of the country in which they are held. Grand Prix competitors are normally invited on the basis of past performance, usually four from each country in each category (male, female, junior and veteran). In addition an 'open' all comers competition with a qualifying standard (about 6c for men, 6b for women) may precede the Grand Prix and the winners may then go on to the Grand Prix itself. Regulars on the Grand Prix circuit have formed an association to look after their interests, the International Professional Climbers Association.

Competition walls should be fifteen metres or more in height and are constructed of wooden or plastic backboards one metre square and covered in a rock-textured coating. The backboards are mounted on a scaffolding structure which allows the degree of overhang of the wall to be adjusted. Each backboard

The first ascent of Big Boys Don't Cry,
Lembert Dome, Tuolumne Meadows,
California

Nicko Mailander on the first free ascent
of Arc en Ciel, Gerbier, Vercors, France

contains a set of holes, five or six, which may be used to attach holds or protection bolts. Holds are small moulded plaques which in theory should be of new design for each competition. In practice, however, there will be a great degree of similarity between the holds encountered on different walls. The climbing is invariably of the 'steep pocketed limestone' style with such features as mantelshelf holds, ledges and cracks invariably absent.

## COMPETITION RULES AND PROCEDURES

Competitions are still a new and developing form of climbing and the rules therefore tend to change quite rapidly and be interpreted rather differently by different organisers. This state of uncertainty has already led to several misunderstandings and misinterpretations of the rules, with consequent argument and appeals. However, the basic structure and competition rules are fairly well determined now, and if these are understood the competitor should have no problem adapting to local variations.

### Competition procedure

Competitors are chosen or invited to U.I.A.A. Grand Prix events but can apply (or be selected on previous climbing standard) for Open Events. Once at the competition the climber registers for the first round by entering an Isolation Zone which keeps the competitor out of sight of the competition wall. The route itself is not unveiled until the Isolation Zone is closed, after which no further registrations are permitted. At registration a draw is made for the order of performance. When the first competitor begins to climb, the second competitor is moved to a Transition Zone, again still out of sight of the wall, where equipment is checked. The competitor is then directed to the Preparation Zone below the route itself for the final three minutes. Timing for the route begins when the competitor's second foot leaves the ground or when the preparation time runs out. The time allowed for the route varies depending on the length of the route and the category of competitor, but is normally about ten minutes.

In open competitions there is normally one event, the Final, with a Super Final if two or more competitors actually complete the final route. In Grand Prix events a semi-final is held to seed the top fifteen competitors for the Final. In the event of two or more competitors succeeding in climbing the Final route, a Super Final is held; if two or more competitors succeed on a Super Final route then they are jointly awarded first place. All other places (rankings) are awarded by measuring the height reached on the route by a competitor before he falls off. Height reached is determined by any hold or wall surface that is touched continuously by the competitor for at least two seconds.

### The rules

Many of the rules are unwieldy and complex, relating mostly to appeals procedures and the like. Only those rules directly related to the climb are given here:

- [ ] Once the ground is left a competitor is not permitted to return. If this happens the competitor is disqualified.

- [ ] A competitor is allowed one attempt only at the route.

- [ ] A competitor may descend at any time during the attempt, but may not re-touch the ground.

- [ ] A competitor's attempt is terminated by the Route Judge who determines the 'highest legitimate point touched' when one of the following occurs:

  1  A fall

  2  The route boundary (marked) is touched or crossed

  3  A competitor fails to clip into protection (deemed to have

happened if the competitor's trailing leg gets above the bolt)

4  If an artificial aid is used

5  If the competitor returns to the ground

6  If the time runs out

☐ In the event of a 'technical fault', e.g. krab not clipped correctly or belay rope too tight and so giving aid, the judge will inform the competitor who may then elect to continue (and perhaps face disqualification) or terminate the attempt and try again after a rest of up to sixty minutes.

☐ A successful completion of the route is determined by the competitor grasping a sling on the final bolt. The competitor then clips in and is lowered off.

☐ Disqualification is incurred if the competitor:

1  Has prior knowledge of the route

2  Gives anyone else prior knowledge

3  Is late for the Isolation Zone closure

4  Fails to appear at the base of the route before the end of the preparation time

5  Uses equipment that does not conform to the regulations (i.e. U.I.A.A. standards)

6  Unropes at any point of the ascent or descent

7  Ignores the instructions of the Route Judge

## TRAINING FOR COMPETITIONS

Training for specific climbing competitions is in many ways much easier to programme and organise than training for rock climbing in general. Competitions occur on predetermined dates and the nature of the activity is much more of a known quantity than real climbing. Because of this it is possible to be much more specific in training, and the 'build-up' and 'peaking' phases can be accurately programmed. Competitions are a two- to three-minute event, very steep and sustained, with most of the work being done by the fingers. A combination of arm/finger strength

*Doing interval training using a self-top-roping system: a tape chest harness helps the prussik device slide up the rope*

training and work on the LA-02 energy system is likely to be the most beneficial training combination — with flexibility work, of course. Interval work can mimic the competition, using a difficult two-minute route on a climbing wall. The interval work should be top-roped with a 'self-roping' system; this consists of a static rope, weighted slightly at the bottom, up which runs a jumaring device (see page 135 Petzl shunts or Cloggers are best). The device is attached to the climber's harness and is held upright and in place by a krab through the device's upper hole attached to a tape loop across the shoulder, or one that is made into a lightweight chest harness. In this way one can safely and easily work out on vertical walls without assistance.

Ideally the wall used for training should be identical to the typical competition wall described previously; familiarity with the properties and characteristics of the backboards and holds is obviously a great advantage. Unfortunately such walls are not yet widely available, but there is nothing to stop groups of climbers purchasing backboards and holds to set up as a training facility for themselves.

Skill training should obviously concentrate on the type of climbing to be encountered in competitions, gently overhanging fingery limestone or sandstone bouldering probably providing the best medium. Well-designed competition routes will be of sustained but even difficulty, rather than having one very hard crux move where everyone falls off. Skill training should therefore concentrate on two or more linked moves rather than the accomplishment of a single move on one hold.

It is almost inevitable that everyone will fall off at some stage in the competition. While the bolt spacing will prevent ground falls and limit fall length to four or five metres, it is still true that many climbers will be unhappy with this prospect. Most climbers who reach this level, however, will almost certainly have had some experience of falling and be able to cope with it. Ideally one should still be frightened of falling to the extent that it motivates one to cling on with great tenacity, but not to the extent that it overtly worries the climber and disrupts his or her skilled performance. Falling training should therefore be aimed at sufficient habituation to overcome the disruptive effects of anxiety, but not so much that falling becomes a carefree activity.

With fixed-date competitions, training should be tapered down to a point five or six days before the competition where strength and LA-02 training should cease. Up to the competition itself training should be light 'overload'. The body is particularly slow to recover from strength and LA-02 work, which may therefore impair competition performance if worked on seriously in the week before competition.

## COMPETITION STRATEGIES

Apart from the obvious ordinary climbing talents required for a competition, the climber can make the best of the situation by the application of one or two extra skills and strategies:

### Gear

Competition equipment rules are still very open to interpretation and clever 'one-upmanship'. Foremost among the possibilities here is the customising of one's boots, adapting them for maximum performance on the particular fifteen metres or so of climbing to be encountered: super sticky rubber with additional resin or rubber softening chemicals (e.g. caustic soda); carbon fibre or fibreglass stiffening implants in your boots or even needle spikes for 'mono doigts' (single-finger holes). All other gear should be stripped down, ultra light and customised for the performance. Quick draws should be on quick release clips on the harness at one end and ready clipped to the rope at the other.

## Warm-up

Competitors are likely to spend some time in the warm-up area waiting for earlier competitors to clear the wall. Some form of pull-up and finger board equipment will normally be provided. This should be used sufficiently to get muscles attuned to the kinds of work expected, but the major part of the warm-up should be concerned with flexibility and whole body warming by light work on the major muscle groups. A regular set warm-up procedure is a good way of concentrating and getting prepared for the climb ahead.

## Preparation

This strategy concerns the accumulation of knowledge about the route to be climbed. Although in most competitions the route will be unseen and you will not see earlier climbers' ascents, there is some foreknowledge that may be useful:

☐ What kind of wall is it and what kind of holds can you expect?

☐ Who is the route planner, what is his style and how tall is he? − a short planner will design routes for short people.

☐ A preparation period is allowed with the competitor in front of the route − use this time to work out as much of the route as possible. Training for competitions could well include some 'route memory and interpretation from the ground' practice. Remember that the time allowed for the route is normally much too long for climbers of average strength, so that some of the climbing time could perhaps be used advantageously for preparation.

☐ Information from previous rounds of the competition regarding route design, hold type and wall angle should all be assimilated as preparation.

## Psyching up for the ascent

Most climbers will find that some psyching-up strategy which concentrates on ignoring the crowd and going out to produce a piece of skilled climbing will be beneficial. The other main worry that competitors report is that of 'not being up to the route'. Here you need to learn to develop (before the competition) confidence in your ability to climb at the grade to be encountered. Anyone who is happy top-roping routes on a wall at 6c should have no difficulty in a 6c competition − the main task, though, is to go out to the competition wall knowing that.

# 14   *Self rescue*

It is essential that the climber learns how to get out of difficulties as he or she learns to climb. Inexperience can lead to all kinds of difficult situations; with a little technique, however, you can learn to extricate yourself from these situations. As you become more experienced, you are likely to find yourself in more difficult situations requiring a higher degree of skill to get out of. With all self-rescue situations the climber should attempt or consider the simplest way out first. If this is not going to work then more complicated manoeuvres may be necessary. This chapter deals with three commonly met situations, though other rarer predicaments can usually be solved by using the same techniques. The most common is when a party finds itself some way up a climb unable to continue because the next pitch is too hard or the weather has changed. Next is the case of a leader who is halfway up a pitch and cannot continue or climb down. Third is the problem encountered when a leader or second falls off and is left dangling on the end of the rope, unable to regain the rock.

All the techniques that follow attempt to use only the kinds of equipment that a climber would normally carry on a route. Perhaps the only items of specialist equipment that the climber should seriously consider carrying are two short 5 mm loops of accessory cord. These loops (prussik loops) are light, cheap and can easily be stashed out of the way; they do, however, make many of the techniques much easier and safer, as well as opening up scope for new techniques. They should be considered essential for the 'multi-pitch climber', while the 'big wall climber' would normally have the mechanical version of prussik loops — clamps or jumars.

## ABSEILING OR RAPPELLING

Abseiling is the simplest way of retreating back down a cliff — in competent careful hands it is a very rapid way of regaining safe ground. In situations of approaching bad weather or darkness speed can be the key factor in safety. Abseiling is often used to retreat from the summit of mountain routes or from climbs that do not reach the top of a cliff but finish at some ledge or other arbitrary point. It is increasingly used as a technique for getting back down a cliff where it is speedier than walking down via an easier but longer route — but this is not really to be recommended as good practice as it greatly increases the risk involved and may also inconvenience other climbers on the cliff.

In its simplest form the abseil rope is doubled, the doubled end being put over a suitable anchor. The single ends are tied with an overhand or figure of eight knot and thrown down the cliff. It is essential to make sure they either reach the ground or another ledge suitable for a further abseil. The classic abseil, little used today, involves putting the ropes from the anchor between the legs, up and diagonally across the front, over the shoulder and down diagonally across the back to the controlling hand. All the friction created by this rope/body contact controls the climber as he descends. Today, however, it is usual to use some kind of friction device or hitch attached to the harness. This is much more comfortable and much safer. The normal options are to use a karabiner brake, Sticht plate, figure of eight descendeur or an Italian hitch; each has its own advantages and disadvantages and all, apart from the figure of eight method, use equipment that is normally carried on an everyday rack.

*The abseil position: feet apart, legs straight, leaning back with the controlling hand low down by the thigh*

of the abseil. When the ground or ledge is reached the last man unties the safety knot at the end of the rope and pulls one end down so that the rope slides round the anchor and is retrieved. This means, of course, that the anchor must be one that the rope will slide around; these are few and far between, trees or pitons being the only usable ones. Usually it is necessary to leave a sling on the anchor and thread the abseil rope through this. The sling should be long enough to clear any sharp bends on the ledge that might prevent the rope being retrieved. Once the sling has had an abseil rope pulled through it, it is probably damaged by the heat generated and should not be used again. For this reason, beware of slings found on anchors.

ABSEILING IS DANGEROUS – It is not technically difficult but there are many small points to watch out for. Meticulous attention to detail is essential for safe abseiling. The following points are *all* important:

☐ Make sure the anchor is sound and the rope will run. The first person down should check that the rope can be pulled down.

☐ Tie a knot in the end if the rope does not reach the ground or if you are not sure. An extra karabiner connected by sling to the main harness should be clipped on to *one* rope. If for

To abseil the climber leans back and puts weight on the rope, preventing the rope sliding by holding on with the control hand (that is, the hand below the abseil device). With feet apart and body turned slightly sideways to look down the control hand side, the climber allows the rope to slide through the control hand and walks backwards down the cliff. The other hand is used as a steadying hand on the part of the rope leading to the anchor. Feet should ideally be flat on the rock in a 'walking' pose; avoid the temptation to stand upright on footholds as this breaks the rhythm any reason the end of the rope is overshot the abseiler will not part company with the rope.

- [ ] Make sure no loose clothing, bits of string or long hair can foul the abseil rope as it passes over you. Very many abseil problems are caused by the device being jammed by foreign objects.

- [ ] The harness karabiner should be a screwgate one with the screw firmly closed and arranged so that it is closest to the right hip − any contact between rope and gate will then tend to tighten the screwgate.

- [ ] Don't bounce or jump, except when crossing overhangs. Jerks on the rope put undue strain on the anchor.

- [ ] If learning to abseil then you should be belayed from the top with a separate safety rope.

- [ ] If possible, don't move sideways: this rubs the rope on any edges above and may well dislodge loose rocks on to you.

- [ ] When the bottom is reached make sure the ropes are untwisted before pulling them down.

- [ ] If the rope jams and you have let go of one end do not climb up the other rope to free it − it may well unjam as you climb up.

- [ ] If the abseil rope is made from two ropes joined by a double fisherman's knot, put the knot on the underneath side of the sling, krab or abseil ring and remember which rope to pull; in all cases it is easier to pull the rope coming out underneath the sling.

- [ ] Carry slings and prussik loops or clamps if there is any chance of the rope not reaching the ground.

It is possible to 'lock' oneself at any point on the abseil by wrapping the control end of the rope around the leg a few times; alternatively the abseil device can be locked properly by tying a couple of half hitches around the tight (up) rope with a bight of the dead rope from below the device.

A Sticht plate locked off during an abseil

Beware inadvertent and almost irrevocable locking of figure of eight descendeurs when the rope running over the waist of the device is flipped over the large ring to form a lark's foot knot. This position can only be retrieved by unloading the device with prussik knots. Inadvertent locking is caused by the rope at the device's waist catching on the rock or, more commonly, by using double ropes where one rope has different properties to the other and becomes slack and twisted as it runs through the figure of eight.

When working in pairs or in a group, a useful safety back-up is for the first person down gently to hold the bottom of the rope. If the abseiler gets out of control the person at the bottom can pull on the rope and so slow down the descent of the abseiler. A further safety precaution, which is rather more difficult to operate, is to slide a loose prussik (or similar) knot down the abseil ropes above the device. This knot is connected to the harness and automatically tightens if the hand which slides the knot is removed. A French prussik is perhaps the best knot to use as it can be released after an inadvertent locking.

## Figure of eight

The figure of eight can be controlled very easily by pulling the control side of the rope downwards to slow the descent. As the control hand is lifted upwards, the rate of descent increases. Locking is easily achieved, crossing the control rope over the device and pulling it down into the gap between figure of eight and rope from above. Both hands are then free for other tasks. Different brands of figure of eight have different descent rates due to their size and surface. Some slippery ones tend to be a little fast for beginners and slip when locked. In such cases the device can be used upside down, i.e. with the rope running through the small ring and the large ring clipped into the waist.

## Karabiner brakes

An abseiling device can be constructed from karabiners, and while this device has more possible parts to go wrong, it can be made from equipment that is used for other things, thus reducing weight. The karabiner brake, as it is called, is formed by passing a rope over the backs of two karabiners clipped onto the main harness karabiner. The screwgate on the harness krab should be close to the left thigh and the gates of the two brake krabs underneath but facing opposite ways. This device, unlike the figure of eight device, does not twist the rope, but it does tend to go a bit fast on steep rock. This problem is usually avoided by the use of a further snaplink krab clipped onto the rope both just

*A karabiner brake using snaplink krabs with gates opposing each other and a third snaplink placed longitudinally to increase friction*

above and just below the upper tip of the harness (screwgate) krab.

## Sticht plate

The Sticht plate makes a good abseil device but it does tend to give a rather jerky descent as it 'snatches' the rope; not good with doubtful anchors or in areas of loose rock. Because the two ropes can be fed through the device at differents rates, this could cause creep over the anchor and result in the two ends of the rope being at unequal height.

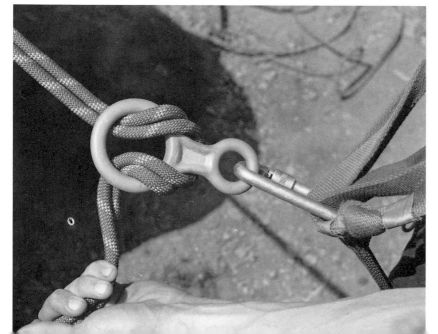

*The figure of eight descendeur in use*

### Italian hitch

A good simple method of abseiling which creates plenty of easily controllable friction. Its main drawback is that is tends to twist the ropes quite badly, especially when the ends are tied together.

### PRUSSIKING

In certain situations it may be necessary to climb up the rope. A leader or second hanging in space, for instance, may need to climb the rope to get out of his predicament. An abseil rope that does not reach the ground or a ledge will have to be re-climbed. A stuck leader can be rescued by hanging a rope from above; if he can climb up the rope the rescue is simple. Prussiking is the name given to any method of climbing a rope using a device that jams itself on to the rope, although the name originally comes from the prussik knot, one of the first rope-climbing knots.

The easiest way to climb a rope is to use one of the mechanical jamming devices on the market such as Jumars, Cloggers or Petzl Ascenders. These devices, used in pairs, with slings attached to stand or sit in, will slide easily up the rope but jam when a downward pull is applied. They are expensive and heavy, but useful when the climber knows he will have a lot of prussiking to do. For the

The Italian hitch

emergency situation one of the very effective prussiking knots will be more useful. A short sling of about half the diameter of the main rope is made into one of these knots around the main rope, long slings are then attached and the whole rig is used in the same way as the mechanical devices. It is therefore useful to carry a couple of short slings of 5 mm rope in your pocket or fastened to a harness for use in such an emergency.

It is worthwhile learning four knots:

- [ ] The prussik knot – the traditional knot that is most useful in straightforward ascent situations.

- [ ] The Klemheist knot – very useful if you have no rope loops, for this knot will work with tape slings.

From top to bottom: the prussik knot, Klemheist knot with sheet bend and Bachmann knot

A Klemheist knot

*A French prussik knot*

☐ The French prussik – a good knot for much self-rescue work because it can be released under load; however, because of this is not so useful for straightforward ascent. Any prussik loop will melt if it is allowed to slide under load down the main rope.

☐ The Bachmann knot – like the French prussik but incorporates a karabiner which is useful as a handle for sliding the knot up the rope. The tendency is, however, for the climber to hang on the krab which causes the knot to slip.

In two-knot prussiking systems the climber can either have his feet in two tapes hanging from the knots and move them up alternately, or both feet can be in the tape from one knot and the other is connected to the waist harness. Both methods require practice before being really effective. In the two-leg loop system the top knot should have an extra safety tape going to the climber's harness or to a chest harness made from tape. In the more useful and common foot-and-sit harness system the sit harness should be connected to the upper knot, so that the climber can sit down and rest as the leg loop knot is slid up the rope. A good deal of experiment and

*A prussik rig*

practice is required to ensure that the loops and slings are the right length to ensure optimum rise with each step up. A problem that is invariably experienced is that the feet have a habit of dropping out of the slings as the knot is moved up. This is best solved by slipping the foot into a clove hitch tied in the end of the sling.

## DEALING WITH PROBLEMS

The two problems most commonly met with are those of what to do with a fallen partner who is suspended on the rope, and how to retreat from cliffs when the abseil rope doesn't reach the ground.

As going downhill is always a preferable solution to a problem, let's look first at the latter situation. In normal conditions and in daylight a party should be able to abseil down a cliff in one rope length, or in several rope lengths taking intermediate belays as they are encountered. On popular big cliffs signs of intermediate anchor points at approximately 45 m intervals will usually be encountered. Some cliffs have special 'descent by abseil' routes. On other cliffs multiple abseils must be treated with great caution and with attention to four important points:

☐ Don't abseil past obvious intermediate ledges just

because you haven't reached the end of the rope.

- [ ] Make sure the rope will pull down before the last person leaves the top anchor.

- [ ] Tie the ends of the rope together.

- [ ] Carry prussik loops and know how to use them.

Abseiling past overhangs is particularly tricky in that it may be difficult to regain the rock below. Mostly this problem can be overcome by instigating a 'swing' at the lip of the overhang then abseiling lower and using the pendulum motion to regain contact with the rock.

A further option in difficult situations that works on a large number of cliffs and in a lot of situations is to tie both ropes together and abseil down the single rope, which has been tied off at the top. This gives ninety metres or so of descent potential and in most crag-climbing situations will ensure that the ground is reached. The rope cannot be retrieved immediately but the party can return later with more equipment and prussik back up the rope to reorganise the situation. Passing the knot on the single rope is simple. Using most figure of eight descendeurs it is possible to abseil straight past a knot tied in 9 mm rope (the most common situation). If brakes, hitches or Sticht plates are used

then the abseiler simply abseils down until the knot jams, then fixes a prussik knot leg loop above the knot. The abseiler then stands in the leg loop and clips his or her harness into the prussik loop. The now unweighted abseil device is reassembled and locked off immediately below the knot. The abseiler then unclips from the prussik knot and steps downwards using the leg loop until the load is taken by the abseil device again – a simple technique that is made much faster and easier with a little practice. This technique is made even faster and easier if a French prussik is used, attached only to the harness. The abseil is stopped just before the knot jams (but only just) by allowing the French prussik to tighten. The descendeur is then repositioned below the knot and weighted again simply by pulling down a hand on top of the French prussik and so releasing the knot.

## Dealing with fallen partners

If possible, prussiking up the rope after a fall should be avoided; it is usually much simpler to be lowered off to the nearest ledge or the ground. A leader who is stuck should try to reverse down to his last runner and be lowered off this, retrieving other intermediate runners as he goes (though only if absolutely sure this top runner is very sound). If he cannot reverse he should try to fix a runner where he is and lower off that. The only other solution is rescue from above.

If a fallen climber decides to prussik, or if the second has to hold his weight on the rope for any length of time, then some way has to be found of taking the weight of the climber off the belayer. This is achieved by the belayer holding the rope with his controlling hand, then fixing a prussik knot on the taut rope with the other. The prussik is connected by a sling to the anchor itself and the belayer then slowly releases the rope so that the anchor takes the strain. The main rope is then tied back to the anchor for safety.

When the Sticht plate is used for belaying it is a simple matter to lock it by tying a couple of half hitches around the live rope with a bight of the dead rope. If the bight is passed through the belay plate krab first this further aids the locking effectiveness. If a direct belay is being used the whole of this 'escaping the system'

*Escaping the system*

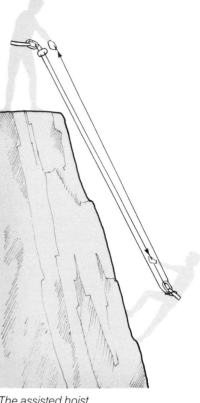

*The assisted hoist*

procedure is much simpler because the belayer is not really 'in the system' in the first place.

Once the belayer has tied back the live rope direct to the anchor he can set about escaping the system, i.e. untying himself from the main rope and anchor so that he is free to move around. Now both climbers can help to sort out the situation. The easiest solution is usually for the fallen climber to prussik up the rope to the stance. Prussik loops can be slid down the rope to the fallen climber or lowered on spare rope (or the

other strand of a 9 mm double rope system). It is possible to prussik using one loop only; this is used for the harness. From a hanging position on this loop the feet are drawn up high and the main rope wrapped around them a couple of times. It is then possible to stand up and slide the harness loop up and so on.

*Assisted hoist* If the fallen climber is unable to prussik then some hauling system must be employed to get the climber to the ledge. An assisted hoist is the easiest option but it requires that the victim is no more than one third of a rope's length below the stance or that there is a spare rope available (again, one strand of a 9 mm pair can be used if it can be untied by the casualty). First the rescuer attaches a French prussik to the live rope close to the belay plate and clips the loop on to the belay plate krab so that when the live rope is pulled up the knot slips, but if the live rope is let out the knot grips – a 'clutch' in other words. Spare rope is then dropped in a loop to the casualty, who clips the loop on to his or her harness loop with a krab. The rescuer then pulls up on the free end while the casualty pulls down on the middle rope (i.e. the only rope that runs downwards). The casualty can be raised easily and rapidly by this method.

*Unassisted hoist*    If the assisted hoist system cannot be used then an unassisted hoist must be employed. First the belayer escapes the system and again, a clutch is set up on the live rope and a further prussik knot attached to the live rope as low down as the rescuer can practicably reach. A loop of the dead rope is clipped to the lower prussik knot and the free end pulled upwards. This raises the live rope which slides through

the clutch. When the lower prussik reaches the clutch the pulling rope is released and the strain is taken by the clutch; the lower prussik is then slid as far down the live rope as possible again and the process repeated.

It will be found that victims can aid matters significantly by 'walking' up the rock. It is virtually impossible to haul someone who cannot help at all if there are obstacles such as overlaps or if the pulley prussik is used on a section of live rope that is running horizontally across a ledge – the pulley really needs to be in a situation where pull direction and the direction of movement of the casualty are the same.

If none of this works then of course you have no option but to leave the victim and go and seek assistance – remember this may only be possible if you are climbing with twin ropes and so have one spare for abseiling.

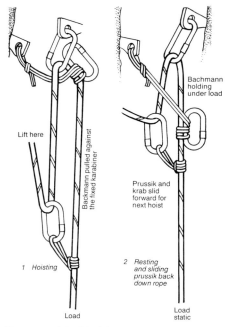

*The unassisted hoist*

# 15    *The environment and ethics*

This chapter is concerned with the responsibilities of the climber to the environment in which he practises his sport and to other climbers who may be affected by his actions. There are no written rules on how climbing is done, and little written on the conduct of climbing; furthermore, climbers are often seen by the general public as irresponsible and antisocial individuals. This may lead the newcomer to climbing to assume that 'anything goes' in the pursuit of the climbing experience; but the environment and the climber's relationship with other climbers are of vital importance in climbing, the setting in which climbing takes place being of especial, if little realised, importance.

## THE CLIMBER AND THE WILDERNESS

Climbing is an environmental sport; the cliffs that pose the challenge are part of our natural environment, the route to the cliffs passes through more of that environment. Nor is the setting of cliffs 'any old natural environment', for it is a feature of cliffs used for climbing that they are to be found in the best of our wilderness areas. It is also a fact that the setting and position of the climb in terms of natural beauty or savage wilderness contributes greatly and inseparably to the climbing experience. Some climbers may

*Climbing is an environmental sport: Cathedral Peak, Sierra Nevada mountains, USA*

not care to admit to the importance of the setting in their climbing experience, competition and the ascent of hard routes being all they see. Even they, however, must be influenced by the strength and emotive power of the wilderness settings of many crags. It is the very scenic isolation and grandeur that gives the routes on high mountain crags such an aura of difficulty.

It goes without saying, then, that climbers, of all people, should appreciate and respect the sanctity of the wilderness in which their sport takes place. Here of course we have the first dilemma — that the act of climbing serves to damage the environment of the very areas the climber professes to care for. Climbers frequent crags in wild areas, creating footpaths on approaches and descent routes, covering the crags in pitons, bolts and discarded bits of tape, not to mention leaving trails of chalk and boot rubber up the rock. With the passage of time, all natural vegetation and loose rock are removed from popular climbs, and some become so worn that they can be spotted from miles away. So climbing itself is not ecologically pure; the very fact that climbing exists means that damage is being done.

Some kind of compromise is necessary, but the important thing for climbers to recognise is that they are in a privileged position so far as access to the wilderness goes, and the nature of the compromise adopted must be one in which the individual climber is thoughtful about the impact of his or her actions. As a general guideline the climber should approach, stop at, and leave the crags doing as little to upset the ecosystem as possible while still practising the sport of climbing. Where there is a choice in what to do the decision should be made with environmental considerations foremost. Litter (including discarded items of protection) is unnecessary and can easily be removed without affecting the climbing. Keeping a low profile visually and orally is obviously not always a priority to the Lycra-clad youths on the popular 'competition' cliffs, but even they should realise that they are at the forefront of climbing's public image. At a time when environmental issues are being taken ever more seriously by growing numbers of people, including politicians, it is important for climbers to command a position of respect as guardians and appreciators of the wilderness.

- ☐ Leave nothing
- ☐ Keep a low profile
- ☐ Change the environment as little as possible

## ACCESS TO ROUTES

Unlike most organised sports, which have facilities created expressly for the participants, climbing relies upon natural features. Access to these cliffs can be problematic, whether the land on which the cliff lies is in public or private ownership. Most climbing depends upon some sort of permissive access; this means that while no-one prevents the climber approaching and climbing on a cliff, he does not have an explicit right to be there. Where cliffs are owned by the nation it is usually because they are in an area of some scenic value; in these situations access is usually monitored in some way or other. Generally speaking, however, climbers have so far managed to maintain fairly free and ready access to crags. That they do so is not unconnected with their image as protectors of the environment, responsible users of the challenges it offers. We have a delicate balancing situation where climbers need to become even more vigilant of their responsibilities towards the environment to keep pace with the growing environmental awareness of those owning or in charge of crags.

In some areas there is a conflict of interest on the crags which has normally been solved by mutual agreement. For instance, crags are frequently used by birds as nesting sites; bird watching or nature conservation groups may consider that climbing should not take place during the breeding season.

A local agreement on access is then worked out with the other interested groups; it is up to climbers to find out if the cliff they intend to climb on is affected by such an agreement, normally by reading the guidebook or climbing magazines or by visiting the local climbing shop.

## CLIMBING ETHICS

These are the unwritten codes of conduct of climbers which dictate (or rather, suggest), how a climber should tackle a climb; they set out the conditions for the sport to be practised. The newcomer to climbing should not be misled by the lack of a written code; the ethics that apply to the activity are well known by all and any violation of the rules is obvious to those about. Ethics are all about the way one climbs, what sort of preparation is permissible beforehand and what kind of equipment can be used.

Some ethics are geared towards conservation of the cliff; keeping it free from defacement; others are concerned with preservation of the essential aspects of rock climbing, i.e. the risk element – the idea of climber and rock unfettered by artificial aids of any kind. The penalties for ignoring such ethics are mostly personal; if you were to use a ladder to ascend a piece of rock it would be obvious to you yourself that it wasn't 'climbing' and that the exercise was pointless. Similarly, the climber should be aware when more subtle codes are bent or broken – if a piece of protection is touched or the rope is kept tight on a downclimbing section, there is again the personal realisation that 'this is not climbing'. No-one seems to mind if a climber, in desperation, grabs a piece of protection for a rest then goes on to complete the climb, though strictly speaking it would have been 'pure' to retreat from the climb and attempt it at some later date. Where problems do arise and reputations are put on the line is when a climber claims to have climbed a route without admitting that certain 'rules' were not followed. This sort of thing results in loss of status among fellow climbers, and at top level leads to angry letters in climbing magazines.

All of this hasn't really answered the question 'What are the ethics; what can I do and what can't I do?' Unfortunately, that is an impossible question to answer, for climbing ethics change either dramatically or subtly from country to country. However, all local variations are really adaptations of the same theme of climbing as naturally as possible and with the use of as little man-made aid as possible. Because climbers do travel regularly from area to area and internationally you need to adjust your approach in a new area, but it is simple enough to find out from other climbers what is normal for the area, and of course no-one will mind if you abide by your own ethics where they are 'more pure' than those of the area being visited.

There seems to be two distinct schools of thought developing on the ethical image of rock climbing. One is the continental European image of rock climbing as a purely gymnastic activity where risk and judgement of risk play little or no part. Falls are possible but bolt protection is placed regularly so that falls do not in general lead to injury. On the other hand, the British and American school of thought places rock climbing within the greater world of mountaineering where risk and its manipulation have always played an intrinsic part in the activity. In these areas, though bolts are occasionally used for protection, one does not find a ladder of bolts beside every route.

No matter where you climb these days the actual ascent of the route is normally described by the term 'red point ascent' or 'red point' (after the German 'Rod punkt', where a red spot was painted on the rock at the foot of routes that had been climbed in one 'go' without protection being touched or used for assistance in any way). In simple terms this means that you can do whatever you like in preparation for a route (e.g. numerous previous attempts or a top-rope ascent), but when

*Mark Leach training on his garage ceiling*

*John Dunne crossing the roof on Breach of the Peace, Malham Cove, North Yorkshire*

*A 200-metre unclimbed sandstone crack in The Arches National Park, Utah*

*Pete Livesey climbing Dream in Cornwall's Great Zawn during the making of the* Rock Athlete *films*

you come to climb it there must be no resting on runners or resting by virtue of falling off on to a runner as these both constitute aid. Many subtle local variations of red pointing now exist, but the original idea is still the most common and would be acceptable in most areas.

## NEW ROUTES

One of the pinnacles of climbing success is the climbing of new routes. This requires skill much greater than that required to follow a guidebook description of an existing route, and of a different nature. The climber has a chance to be creative, to see the line of a possible route or an unclimbed piece of rock and to climb it, then name the route. The route is his own, a lasting statement of that climber's style and creativity. Royal Robbins, a leading American climber, sums up the climbing of new routes very aptly: 'New routes are creations combining line and style.' By that he means that the leader's creativity in spotting the line must be matched by the style in which he climbs the route, that is according to the generally accepted ideas in that area.

In many areas, for instance, it is usual for would-be new routers to practise all the moves of a new route for several days on a top rope before attempting to lead the route.

This results in a route that is much harder for subsequent ascentionists and much harder than one which was climbed genuinely 'on sight'. In other areas the 'on sight' ascent is the norm; a climber sights and works out a line, then starts from the bottom to lead the route straight away. Again, in some areas many attempts and techniques such as 'hang dogging' may be employed, while in others a fall or rest on runners means that the climber has failed and must return at another date to try again.

*Soloing – just climber and rock*

## SOLOING

Soloing is climbing a route without a rope or equipment other than clothing and boots. Like extended bouldering, the commitment involved is ultimate; absolute confidence in technique and ability is required to carry out this highly developed climbing art. Condemned by many as foolhardy, but seen by as many more as being the purest and best form of climbing, soloing attracts but a few who can successfully enjoy the total commitment and freedom involved. What is certain is that soloing for its participants is the most invigorating form of climbing possible; just climber and rock, with talk of cheating and ethics completely meaningless.

# 16 *What now?*

Once the basic skills of leading climbs have been mastered, the whole world of rock climbing is open to the young climber.

Progress is possible in a variety of directions. For those who wish to improve technically there is an ever-increasing store of hard outcrop and crag climbs for the climber to work up to. The top grades are continually being extended and the number of climbers doing routes at these top grades is increasing. Even to the experienced rock climber, the sheer difficulty of the hardest climbs is sometimes difficult to comprehend. There is certainly plenty of scope here for the aspiring 'tiger'. Internationally there are bigger cliffs and mountains offering superb rock climbing experiences in tremendous surroundings. Here the sheer technical difficulty of the shorter outcrop climbs is found along with long rock climbs in serious situations amid grand mountain scenery – the ultimate in climbing experiences. Certainly everyone should try it; there are routes for climbers of all standards. The snow and granite peaks of the Western Alps, the limestone towers of the Eastern Alps, or the long technical routes reminiscent of Welsh climbing to be found in the Maritime Alps; all offer beautiful climbs that will test climbers of all grades. Stamina, experience, drive or 'push' all play a part in the successful completion of this type of climb.

Some climbers will graduate to the greater world of mountaineering where the rock difficulties are equally matched by the problems presented by the weather, altitude, remoteness and snow and ice conditions. Here the climber becomes a true explorer and the remoteness is all-important. The objective is usually a summit by the easiest route; though 'the easiest' is never easy.

Whatever 'game' the individual climber takes up does not matter; some climbers specialise in crag climbing or even bouldering while others are big wall experts where 'space walking' situations are the norm. Most climbers, however, do not specialise but take every opportunity to engage in all branches of the sport. Whatever your preference, the best experiences are most frequently found in travel to new and exciting climbing areas in different regions of your own country or more commonly abroad. Different rock, different styles of climb, different climbers, different climate and above all a whole new and inspiring scenic setting for the activity are some of the pleasures of international rock climbing. The real explorers will want something extra, such as to visit rock faces in little-known regions that are distinctly hard to reach – places like Baffin Island, Patagonia and the Hoggar Mountains of the Sahara are typical examples.

## WHERE TO CLIMB

This chapter is intended to give the climber some idea of what is available in the world of rock climbing. Far from being an exhaustive list, it is merely a selection of the world's well-known crag and big wall areas, together with a few of the lesser-known areas for the explorers. There are twenty-two countries, listed first, where both climbing and climbers form a significant group; these are the front-line climbing countries. Other countries, while having very few climbers, do have significant climbing areas and scope for development.

## British Isles

*North Wales*  Climbs of up to 200 m, traditionally one of the world's climbing centres. Mostly metamorphic rock, some limestone on the coast. Llanberis is the main centre.

*Lake District*  The other historic centre of rock climbing. Thousands of climbs up to 150 m. Metamorphic and volcanic rock. Langdale, Wasdale and Borrowdale are the main centres.

*Peak District*  Thousands of gritstone and limestone outcrop climbs. Home of some of the world's hardest technical climbs.

*Yorkshire*  A less freqented gritstone and limestone outcrop area with nevertheless many fine routes including most of the hardest limestone climbs in the world. Together with the Peak District, the home ground of most of Britain's leading climbers.

*Cornwall*  An area of superb granite sea cliffs and remote coastal scenery. Excellent climbs up to 100 m and good weather.

Pembrokeshire, Devon and Northumberland have significant sea cliff areas while Sussex, Leicestershire, Cheshire, Lancashire and Northumberland all have popular outcrops. Mention should also be made of the large limestone cliffs found in Somerset, South Wales and the Wye Valley, all of which have long classic routes.

*Scotland*  A land of rock in its northern half: unfortunately it is also

*Malham Cove, North Yorkshire: the biggest concentration of the world's hardest limestone routes*

a land of rain, snow, deep heather and vegetation which does limit its potential somewhat. Nevertheless the cliffs are sometimes huge by British standards and the situations remote and beautiful. Key areas are Skye with the Cuillin range and its sea cliffs; Glencoe and Ben Nevis in the western Highlands; the big granite cliffs of the East and West Cairngorms (Creag an Dubh Loch and the Shelter Stone) and the remote cliffs of the far north such as Carnmore where long walks and quite unbelievably beautiful settings are the main attractions.

*Ireland* Somewhat like Scotland; a lot of rock but rather undeveloped and vegetated. The sea cliffs are probably best, with the large and difficult Fair Head being most important while the limestone of Clare is more amenable. Glendalough is best known of the inland areas, though there are numerous local 'cragging' and bouldering outcrops.

*Les Calanques: easy climbing above the sea*

## France

France probably has more developed rock and climbing choice than any other country in the world. Its climate is excellent for climbing and access to areas and cliffs is normally very easy. The north and west contains mostly low granite, sandstone and limestone outcrop and bouldering cliffs, while the Alps in the far east of the country contain all the high granite routes with bad weather potential and serious approach problems. Just west of the Alps lie the slightly lower ranges of the pre-Alps and it is here that the vast wealth of France's big rock routes lie:

*Aiguilles Rouge*   Granite peaks just west of Chamonix.

*Chartreuse*   Tower-like limestone plateaux with 400 m cliffs north of Grenoble.

*Vercors*   Superb limestone area (up to 500 m) with good weather, just south of Grenoble.

*Salève*   Geneva's local mountain, limestone up to 150 m high.

*Verdon Gorge*   One of the world's best climbing areas developed entirely since 1974; a limestone gorge with roads at the top but not at the bottom and routes of up to 350 m.

*Buoux*   A cult limestone cliff in Vaucluse with 100 m routes and some of the most difficult single pitches in the world.

*Sainte Victoire*   A smooth limestone slab with rock of unbelievable quality and some scary climbing.

*Les Calanques*   Limestone sea cliffs in fjord-like inlets; beautiful settings with superb rock and hundreds of classic reasonably graded climbs. Can be crowded.

*Caroux*   A mountain and gorge in Languedoc littered with crags of volcanic rock with excellent weather and routes of all grades.

## Switzerland

Often thought of as purely a snowy alpine country but is actually a place with more rock climbing potential than most European countries. Superb mountain rock climbing is to be found in many parts, but the best known areas are the granite of Salbitschijen, the Bregaglia and the limestone of the Kingspitz. Giant granite slabs in the Grimsel Valley are now well developed with routes of up to 300 m.

Less well known are the beautiful limestone ridges of the Alpstein and Bockmattli areas, with clean mountain limestone of great quality.

*Nicko Mailander on Grade VII climbing on the granite walls of the Salbitschijen area of eastern Switzerland*

## Italy

Italy has two distinct aspects: the limestone towers of the Dolomites are truly alpine but rapidly developing as a free climbing area with routes of up to 1200 m. Outcrop climbing has taken off in Italy now, with granite walls and slabs in valleys running south from the Alps (Mello, Arco). Limestone crags in the south-western tip of northern Italy (Finale Ligure) are for the most part undeveloped (except at Finale) but offer great potential.

## Federal Republic of Germany

Across the southern half of Germany are to be found the sandstone tower outcrops of the Rheinlandpflatz, the limestone riverside cliffs of the Donautal and the limestone crags of the Frankenjura. On the Austrian border are three major big wall rock areas in the limestone peaks of the Wetternhorn (600 m), the loose Karwendal range (1000 m) and the beautiful landscape and rock of the underdeveloped Berchtesgarten Alps (500 m routes).

*The Spigolo Giallo (E1), Tre Cime, in the Italian Dolomites*

## Austria

Austria's main rock climbing areas are the two impressive limestone mountain areas of the Kaisergebirge and Dachstein ranges. The Kaisergebirge especially is a dramatic area of sharp peaks and bare clean rock with a concentrated wealth of longish routes.

## German Democratic Republic

The main rock climbing areas are the sandstone outcrops of the Elbe Valley near Dresden. Climbs of all grades, some extremely difficult.

## Belgium

A fine rock-climbing area is to be found in the Ardennes. The limestone cliffs of Freyr are best known, with many good routes of up to 120 m.

## Norway

A country of rock and water with many excellent rock-climbing areas, notably the Romsdal Valley and the granite peaks of Northern Norway, such as Stetind near Tromso. Climbs in the Romsdal are among the longest rock climbs in Europe, some being nearly 2000 m long. Outcrop climbing is also well developed around the main centres of population such as Oslo.

*The 400 m limestone towers of the Predigstuhl, Kaisergebirge, Austria*

## Spain

An emergent rock-climbing area with the traditional limestone sub-alpine peaks of the Picos D'Europa in the north now complemented by the limestone sea cliffs of the Mediterranean coastline and gorges just inland. Quality granite outcrops are also developed in the Sierra Nevada.

## Sweden

Sweden has several well-developed glacially scoured granite outcrops, mainly close to Stockholm and Gothenberg, with little use made so far of the bigger cliffs of the north.

## Yugoslavia

The northern mountains are limestone and rocky (Triglav and surrounding peaks) but not terribly well developed for rock climbing. More recently limestone gorges inland from Trieste and Split have been developed, giving some classic modern routes of up to 200 m.

## Greece

The Vicos Gorge of northern Greece is probably the largest undeveloped limestone cliff of Europe (400+ m), while the limestone sea cliffs of Varassova on the Gulf of Corinth are large and unusual. Athens has developed outcrops on good rock while the south offers unlimited small limestone cliffs for the explorer.

## Czechoslovakia

Two main areas, a series of substantial limestone outcrops in the karst area of the Low Tatra and a group of sandstone towers similar to those in the Elbe valley in the German Democratic Republic.

## Russia

Much of Russia's rock climbing is aimed at competition climbing with much less in the way of recorded routes being evident. The best-known areas are in the Crimea, especially around Yalta on the Black Sea.

## U.S.A.

There are several vibrant and important rock-climbing areas in this land of tremendous natural rock features. Undoubtedly the foremost area is the often unfairly berated Yosemite Valley, a mecca for all kinds of rock climbing on some of the cleanest and best granite in the world. There are

*Climbing on the Three Brothers, Yosemite Valley*

thousands of routes of all styles up to 1000 m in length. The only problems seem to be the heat in midsummer and local bureaucracy. In the high country just east of Yosemite are the remarkable Tuolomne Meadows, a large area of bare rock and pine trees interspersed with delightful alpine meadows at an altitude of 2500 m. Glaciated 'domes' of granite give superb routes of all grades while the sharper mountainous spires give classic easy routes at high altitude. To the south Mount Whitney has excellent remote big wall routes at very high altitude. All in all, the Sierra Nevada range running down the west side of the U.S.A. must contain much of the world's finest rock and routes.

*The Desert*   The desert states of Utah, Arizona, New Mexico, Colorado and Nevada contain many remote and not so remote areas of sandstone cliffs, many in areas of dramatic isolated towers and canyons.

*Colorado*   A mountain state with a very active rock-climbing scene which ranges from climbing on the classic outcrops of Eldorado Canyon near Boulder to the big serious 'Painted Walls' of Black Canyon and the high alpine Diamond Face of Longs Peak in the Rocky Mountains National Park.

*The north-west face of Fairview Dome (5.9), Tuolomne Meadows, California*

*Shawangunks* The major rock-climbing centre of the eastern states (but not the only one by any means), which lies in the Adirondack Mountains in New York State. Steep outcrops up to 100 m high are well developed and easily accessible – similar in many ways to British outcrop climbing.

Many other areas of note exist, particularly the remote big wall routes of Wyoming's Wind Rivers area and the rock faces of Alaska.

## Canada

A vast country with several widely spread rock areas, with the accent on high quality big wall routes in remote alpine settings – indeed, after Patagonia, Canada is probably the best venue in the world for seeking remote rock in breathtaking settings.

*Bugaboos* Beautiful granite peaks in an alpine setting in the Rockies, with many fine rock climbs.

*Squamish Chief* Near Vancouver, a 600 m cliff with several difficult rock climbs.

*Calgary* One of Canada's main climbing centres, with many large limestone cliffs close by as well as the peaks of the Rockies themselves.

*Logan Range* Situated in the North-West Territories and accessible by float plane or helicopter, this range contains many granite faces including the classic Lotus Flower Tower.

*Baffin Island* A large and remote arctic island with a peninsular of granite peaks in the east dominated by the superb granite spire of Mount Asgard. Quite an accessible area considering its remote position.

## Australia

A major rock-climbing nation with the emphasis almost entirely on crag climbing. Many highly developed outcrop areas with climbs of up to 400 m in Queensland, New South Wales, Victoria and Tasmania. The best-known outcrops are Frog Buttress, Buffalo Gorge, Frenchman's Cap and Arapiles. Climbs of all standards up to the hardest technical grades.

## New Zealand

Mainly an alpine country, but with one or two pockets of outcrop climbing, mainly in the North Island. Longer routes of twelve to fifteen pitches are to be found in the Darren range towards the southern end of South Island.

## Japan

A country with a strong alpine tradition but with a surprising amount of rock-climbing activity in the country itself. The best areas are mostly shortish granite outcrops and boulders.

Many other countries have little or nothing in the way of local rock-climbing scenes but they do have excellent rock-climbing areas. Mention should be made of:

*Algeria* The desert rock towers of the Hoggar Mountains.

*Patagonia* On the Chile-Argentina border in the far south – incredible rock towers with lots of weather.

*Jordan* Red desert sandstone up to 500 m in height.

*Egypt* The walls of Mount Sinai give long routes on mediocre rock.

*Kenya* Longish crag routes in places like Hell's Gate Gorge, complete with killer bees.

*Greenland* A couple of big wall rock climbing areas have been climbed so far.

*Karakoram (Central Asia)* Many rock walls and towers here at a lower altitude than the main peaks which are only just being developed, but obviously have great potential in the big wall climbing sphere.

# 17 *Information and organisations*

## THE BRITISH MOUNTAINEERING COUNCIL

The B.M.C. is the representative body of mountaineering in Britain, fulfilling an important but difficult role. Elected from British clubs, the council seeks to further the interests of British climbers in many fields such as guidebooks, grants to expeditions, technical advice, training advice, access to crags and co-operation with climbers from other countries. Much to the relief of climbers in general, the B.M.C. does not seek to govern them, but wisely realises they are ungovernable and so seeks only to help them. Most clubs are affiliated or you can become an individual member. The address is:

> British Mountaineering Council
> Precinct Centre
> Booth Street East
> Manchester M13 9RZ

They will have the addresses of the climbing clubs in your area.

For the individual climber the B.M.C. can offer help in several important ways. For the beginner it produces basic safety advice booklets and technical booklets on basic equipment. It offers advice on clubs to join and recognised courses that can be attended. Indeed the B.M.C. runs each year a series of courses in rock climbing, summer and winter mountaineering and Alpine climbing aimed at the beginner and intermediate. Access to crags is an increasing problem and the B.M.C., via its area committees and access officer, is usually very well informed about any problems in your area or on a particular cliff you may wish to visit. The B.M.C. also has excellent international contacts, both with individuals and other climbing organisations, which can be of great help when visiting more exotic climbing areas. A further important service is that of arranging insurance for rock climbers and mountaineers – very useful in that it covers the requirements of participants in a 'high risk' sport who actually rarely get hurt but who are forever misplacing baggage and equipment.

## CLIMBING COURSES

As well as the B.M.C. courses, there are dozens of organisations and companies offering rock-climbing courses at various levels which aim either to instruct or simply to guide. Outstanding among these courses are those run by the National Mountain Activities Centre at Plas y Brenin in North Wales, close to the heart of Britain's premier rock-climbing area. Other courses may be run by commercial organisations or individuals; in all cases one should ensure that the instructor is a qualified guide (holder of the Association of British Mountain Guides *carnet*) or a qualified instructor (holder of the Mountaineering Instructor's Certificate). The Association of British Mountain Guides are an independant organisation of professional guides who undergo substantial testing to gain their guide's status, while the Mountaineering Instructor's Certificate is at a similar level and is a similarly tested award for rock climbing and mountaineering.

## BOOKS, GUIDEBOOKS AND MAGAZINES

Rock climbing has a wealth of literature, both of the factual, topographic descriptive type and the epic narrative type. Good climbing shops are the best place to find these books, as few of the bookstore chains stock the best ones. Besides literally thousands of area guidebooks there are several dozen superbly illustrated large-format guides which cover the best routes at a particular level in any one country, region or group of cliffs. Guidebooks for less well-known areas will probably have to be purchased from climbing shops in that area or ordered via your local shop.

There are several climbing magazines in English with various emphases:

*Mountain*   An international rock and mountain climbing magazine.

*High*   A mostly British rock-climbing magazine with some mountaineering and other related activities.

*Climber and Hillwalker*   Similar to *High*.

*On The Edge*   A purely British rock-climbing magazine but with features on rock everywhere.

*Climbing*   An Amercian magazine with a large circulation and a reputation for illustrations and issues, both American and international.

*Rock and Ice*   Similar to *Climber*.

*Wild*   An Australian publication with mostly Australian rock climbing features.

## Reference books

For useful further reading on specific areas of rock climbing the following books are recommended:

## General mountaincraft

Alan Blackshaw, *Mountaineering* (Penguin, 1973)
Eric Langmuir, *Mountaincraft and Leadership* (Mountain Walking Leader Training Board, 1984)

## Self rescue

Bill March, *Modern Rope Techniques in Mountaineering* (Cicerone, 1976)
Nigel Shepherd, *Self Rescue Techniques for Climbers and Instructors* (Adventure Unlimited, 1988)

## Technical information

B.M.C. Technical Committee, *Belaying* (B.M.C., 1989)
B.M.C. Technical Committee, *Knots* (B.M.C., 1986)
B.M.C. Technical Committee, *Ropes* (B.M.C., 1987)

## Training

Per Astrand and Kaare Rodhl, *A Textbook of Work Physiology* (McGraw Hill, 1977)
B.M.C. Training for Rock Climbing Committee, *Rock Fit* (B.M.C., 1989)
E. L. Fox and F. K. Mathews, *The Physiological Basis of P.E. and Athletics* (Saunders, 1976)
Martyn Hurn and Pat Ingle, *Climbing Fit* (Crowood, 1988)
J. Syer and C. Connolly, *Sporting Body, Sporting Mind* (Cambridge University Press, 1984)

# 18 Climbing terms and grades

Climbers' conversations are full of climbing terms and odd slang expressions. This short glossary contains only the most important words; the rest you will pick up rapidly as you mix with other climbers.

## ROPEWORK

*Anchor* The rock feature e.g. spike, block or chockstone, or the piton, bolt or nut on to which the climber fastens himself in order to belay.

*Belay* To 'belay' is to hold the rope to protect the leader or second.

*Belayer* The person holding the rope – a very important person.

*I'm belayed* or *on belay* The shout the leader gives to tell his second he is safely tied on and ready for the second to climb.

*Lead* To go up the climb first, clipping your trail rope to protection that you place as you progress. The other end of the rope is belayed by the second.

*Leading through* When the second arrives at a stance, then continues to lead the next pitch and so becomes the leader.

*Pitch* A long climb is split into natural sections between ledges where the climber stops and brings up the second person. This section is a pitch.

*Protection* Equipment like nuts, tapes, bolts or pitons placed on a pitch and connected to the rope with a karabiner to limit the length of a leader's possible fall. Also called a 'runner'.

*Rap down* or *'Ab off'* Slang expressions meaning to abseil or rappel, i.e. to slide down the rope to descend from the crag or mountain.

*Rope length* Means that the pitch is as long as a normal rope, that is about 45 m.

*Stance* The ledge is at the end of a pitch where the leader anchors himself before bringing up the second person.

*Thread* A type of anchor where the rope or a sling must be threaded behind a jammed block or through an 'eyehole'.

## EQUIPMENT

*Bolts* Expansion bolts with a hanger that takes a karabiner are used in certain areas in place of nuts and pegs. They need a hole drilled in the rock and are thereafter permanent fixtures.

*Camming nuts* An expanding nut that has moving spring-loaded cams that grip the sides of smooth or outward-flaring cracks.

*Kernmantel* The most common kind of climbing rope used today, 11 mm in diameter or 9 mm if used double. It has a plaited outer sheath (the *mantel*) and slightly twisted filaments for the core (the *Kern*). It is made of Nylon or Perlon (the German word for Nylon). Hawser-laid rope is the other, less common, type, formed from three main strands twisted together.

*Krab* A karabiner, an oval-shaped piece of aluminium with a snap shut gate on one side, used for connecting the main rope to a belay sling or runner. If used on the waist, harness or main belay it should be a screwgate, that is a krab with a screwed sleeve to lock the gate closed.

*Lycra*    After the rope, the second most important piece of equipment for the 'hot shot' – 'Lycras' are tights in ever more outrageous colour schemes.

*Nuts*    Also called chocks and wedges. Lumps of wedge-shaped aluminium threaded with a wire or rope loop, used for anchors on main or running belays. Placed in cracks.

*Pegs*    If nuts will not fit in a crack, then pegs (pitons, steel spikes) are used for belays. You will need a peg hammer to place them.

*Sling*    A loop of rope, usually between 1 m and 3 m long and tied with a double fisherman's knot. Normally made from 9 mm or 11 mm Kernmantel rope and used for belays and runners.

*Sticky boots*    Modern rock-climbing boots have a smooth sticky rubber sole that helps you stick to the rock – it also collects sand, dust and dead flies.

*Tape*    A sling made of Nylon tape, useful for sliding into thin cracks behind blocks and spikes.

## ROCK AND ITS FEATURES

*Chimney*    A crack wide enough to get into.

*Chockstone*    A lump of rock jammed in a crack, chimney or gulley.

*Corner*    A more pronounced groove, with the walls at right-angles to each other like the inside of an open book.

*Gully*    A large deep chimney or corner.

*Hold*    Non-climbers call them 'grips', anything to put your hands or feet on. Different types are 'jugs' (big handholds), side holds, handholds, undercuts, etc.

*Groove* or *diedre*    A depression running up the face, frequently with a crack in the back.

*Manky*    Describes loose or dirty rock; a manky runner is a poor or loose running belay.

*Niche*    A small depression in the rock face, usually a resting place.

*Overhang, roof, bulge*    All terms to describe rock that juts out over your head.

*Rib* or *arete*    A steep ridge of rock on a cliff or mountain.

*Slab*    A low-angled area of rock; sometimes you can climb it on friction alone.

*Wall*    A steeper area of rock than a slab, usually less than vertical, but one that always feels more than vertical when you are climbing on it!

*Way off*    The route down from the top of the crag; it is best to know where it goes before you get up there.

## CLIMBING MOVES

*Aid*  Climbed with the aid of slings, nuts, pitons or bolts, sometimes for just one move on an otherwise free climb, sometimes for whole routes.

*Bold*  A climb or pitch with few runners to protect the leader.

*Bridging* or *stemming*  Climbing with hands or feet (or both) wide apart on opposite walls of a corner or chimney.

*Crank*  A straight brute-force pull-up on the arm(s) to gain height to reach the next hold.

*Crux*  The most difficult move or moves on a climb.

*Dyno*  A real leaping move for a hold which you hope is there.

*Epic*  A real unforeseen adventure on a climb.

*Free*  Climbed without help from slings, nuts, pitons or bolts.

*Gripped*  What you are when you get scared at a very hard move, until you finally do it or retreat.

*Jamming*  Climbing by jamming or wedging hands, fingers, arms, feet or legs into a crack.

*Layback*  A way of climbing a crack in a corner by pulling on the edge of the crack with the hands and walking up the opposite wall with the feet.

*Lock*  To lock certain muscles, usually biceps or triceps, in one position so that the other arm may be taken off and a new hold reached.

*Move*  An individual step or movement on a climb.

*Red pointing*  Style of hard, free climbing where the ultimate aim is to climb a route without falling or otherwise touching or using the protection.

*Route*  A climb.

*Shake out*  When muscles get 'pumped' (fatigued) the lactic acid in them disperses more quickly if the limbs are hung and shaken.

*Slap*  A lunge for a hold where the friction of the palm on the rock helps in reaching the hold; common among beginners and hot shots.

*Smear*  To place your sticky boots on smooth rock and hope you make the move before the boot slides off.

*Thin*  A section of climb on small holds, delicate.

## GRADES OF CLIMBS

All climbs are graded for difficulty and seriousness; this is usually done by the members of the first ascent party and perhaps modified later by the guidebook writers. Most climbs appear in a guidebook of some form or other, varying from a duplicated pamphlet or a full-scale book.

The guidebooks cover anything from one cliff to a complete climbing area. There are two kinds of grade in Britain; an adjectival grade and a numerical one. The adjectival grade gives an overall impression of both the difficulty and seriousness of a route. The grades are:

| | |
|---|---|
| Easy | E |
| Moderate | Mod. |
| Difficult | Diff. |
| Very difficult | V. Diff. |
| Severe (sometimes prefixed by 'mild' or 'hard') | S |
| Very severe | VS |
| Hard very severe | HVS |
| Extremely severe | XS |

Extremely severe is then subdivided into E1, E2, E3, etc.

As you can see, the guide writers have run out of adjectives, with the result that the upper grades have become crammed with routes of a wide range of difficulty. The grades at the lower end have less meaning in modern rock climbing, Diff. and V. Diff. being quite easy climbs.

The numerical grade applies to

individual pitches and is open-ended, i.e. the more difficult the pitches get, the higher the number used to describe them. The numerical grade applies only to the actual technical difficulty and perhaps the strenuousness of a pitch (it is difficult to separate the two).

The grades are (so far):

1a, b or c
2a, b or c
3a, b or c
4a, b or c
5a, b or c
6a, b or c
7a, b or c

Pitches on climbs of Severe and below are not usually given numerical grades, consequently numbers 1, 2 and 3 are never used. 4a to 5a are usually found on VS climbs, 4a to 5c on HVS climbs and 4c to 7c on XS climbs.

If a climb is HVS and 5c, this tends to indicate that it is well protected by runners and therefore not very serious. However, if a climb is 5a and E3 it should be quite serious, either bold runnerless climbing, loose rock or poor belays.

A beginner would normally start on Moderates, Diffs., or V. Diffs. How fast he progresses after that depends on the climber. Some people are leading E-graded climbers after three months' climbing, others enjoy going no further than Severe in all their climbing career.

*A table of comparative international rock climbing grades*

| UIAA Grades | French Grades | USA Grades | British Grades | Australian Grades | German Grades |
|---|---|---|---|---|---|
| I | 1 | 5.2 | moderate | | I |
| II | 2 | 5.3 | difficult | 11 | II |
| III | 3 | 5.4 | very difficult | 12 | III |
| IV± | 4 | 5.5 | 4a | 13 | IV |
| V− | 5 | 5.6 | 4b | | V |
| V | | 5.7 | | 14 | VI |
| V+ | | | 4c | 15 | VIIa |
| VI− | 5+ | 5.8 | 5a | 16 | |
| | | | | 17 | VIIb |
| VI | 6a | 5.9 | 5b | 18 | VIIc |
| VI+ | 6a+ | 5.10a | | 19 | |
| VII− | 6b | 5.10b | | 20 | VIIIa |
| | | 5.10c | 5c | 21 | |
| VII | 6b+ | 5.10d | | | VIIIb |
| VII+ | 6c | 5.11a | | 22 | VIIIc |
| VIII− | 6c+ | 5.11b | 6a | 23 | IXa |
| | 7a | 5.11c | | 24 | IXb |
| VIII | 7a+ | 5.11d | | 25 | IXc |
| VIII+ | 7b | 5.12a | 6b | | Xa |
| | 7b+ | 5.12b | | 26 | |
| IX− | | 5.12c | | | Xb |
| IX | 7c | 5.12d | 6c | 27 | |
| | 7c+ | 5.13a | | 28 | Xc |
| IX+ | 8a | | | 29 | |
| | 8a+ | 5.13b | | 30 | |
| X− | | 5.13c | 7a | 31 | |
| X | 8b | | | 32 | |
| | 8b+ | 5.13d | | | |
| X+ | 8c | 5.14a | 7b | 33 | |